SKY
BATTLES

SKY BATTLES

DRAMATIC AIR
WARFARE ACTIONS

ALFRED PRICE

CASSELL

First published by Arms and Armour Press 1993
This Cassell Military Classics edition 1998

Cassell Plc
Wellington House, 125 Strand, London WC2R 0BB

Reprinted 2000

British Library Cataloguing-in-Publication Data: a catalogue
record for this book is available from the British Library

ISBN 0-304-35103-2

Edited and designed by Roger Chesneau
Printed and bound in Great Britain by
Cox & Wyman Ltd., Reading, Berks.

Cover illustration: *Dorniers Attacking Kenley*
by Mark Postlewaite, GAVA. Reproduced by courtesy
of the artist.

Cassell Military Classics are available from all good bookshops
or from:

Cassell C.S.
Book Service By Post
PO Box 29, Douglas I-O-M
IM99   1BQ
telephone: 01624 675137, fax: 01624 670923

Contents

Introduction

MY AIM IN WRITING this work has been to illustrate the actuality of aerial warfare during the past eight decades, by bringing together a series of detailed accounts of air actions spread throughout the period. To portray the multi-faceted nature of the air weapon, the narratives that follow include descriptions of each of the main roles in which aircraft are employed in time of war.

Chapter 1, 'Above the Fields of France', provides a rare insight into fighter operations over the Western Front during the final year of the First World War. Major William Sholto Douglas commanded No 84 Squadron equipped with S.E.5A fighters, and the account is based on a tactical paper that he wrote and also on the unit's records. Following painful lessons learned when the Squadron entered combat, its commander worked out his tactical doctrine almost from first principles. Douglas himself was not a high scorer in combat, but thanks to his tactical leadership his squadron became one of the most effective air fighting units of its time. The techniques he formulated enabled others, notably Captain Andrew Beauchamp Proctor VC, to amass large victory scores while avoiding the risks that eventually claimed the lives of so many successful pilots. No 84 Squadron was continually in action throughout the final twelve months of the conflict, fighting over one of the most active parts of the battle front. Yet, after the first three weeks, the unit suffered relatively few losses.

The Second World War, which began in September 1939, was the first major conflict in which the possession of air superiority allowed one side to impose major constraints on operations by the opposing land and sea forces. Chapter 2, 'The Rise and Demise of the Stuka', describes a type of operation that was relatively easy for the side that possessed air superiority and hazardous if that quality had been lost. During the early *Blitzkrieg* campaigns in Poland, Norway, Belgium, Holland and France, the Junkers Ju 87 'Stuka' dive-bombers attacked targets with pin-point accuracy to support the German armoured thrusts. The Stukas tried to continue their run of successes during the Battle of Britain in the summer of 1940, and although they inflicted severe damage on their targets they suffered heavy losses in the process. Against warships manoeuvring in open water the dive-bombers remained a potent threat, until the vessels were provided with sufficiently strong air cover to make such attacks unproductive.

From time to time an air attack goes terribly wrong, and as a result the raiding force pays a terrible price. Chapter 3, 'Only One Came Back', and Chapter 4, 'Low Altitude Attack', provide examples of a couple of small-scale actions in which the raiders were all but wiped out.

By the autumn of 1940 the *Luftwaffe* had come to the realization that the only way it could mount a sustained air attack on strategic targets in Great Britain was to send its bombers under cover of darkness. Chapter 5, 'Countering the Night Bomber', describes the first large-scale night bombing campaign in history. Initially the raiders suffered minimal losses, but gradually the night defences improved and by the end of the period they had started to take an increasingly heavy toll.

At sea, one notable development during the Second World War was that the aircraft carrier ousted the battleship as the primary instrument of surface naval power. When opposing carrier forces went into action against their own kind the result was a complex interplay between air and naval forces, and the first such encounter, in May 1942, is described in Chapter 6, 'Battle of the Coral Sea'.

Another air campaign that had features quite unlike any other is described in Chapter 7, 'Battle of the Bay'. 'The Bay' was the Bay of Biscay, and the actions were between submarine-hunting aircraft of Royal Air Force Coastal Command on the one side and German U-boats on the other. During this campaign air crews logged vast numbers of flying hours but only rarely did they see anything of their enemy. In parallel with the air–sea battle there ran an equally important struggle between the opposing sides' technicians, with each trying to outwit the other. During the summer of 1943 the strategic bombardment of targets in Germany by US heavy bombers entered its critical phase, with the action described in Chapter 8, 'The Regensburg Strike'. Then it became clear that the defensive firepower from formations of heavily armed Flying Fortresses was insufficient to deter attacks from a determined and well-equipped enemy fighter force. The answer was to push ahead with the development of the long-range escort fighter, with results that will be observed in later chapters.

Reconnaissance is a vitally important aspect of air power. Yet, because it involves single aircraft which seek to avoid combat, there is usually little action and the subject receives less attention than it deserves. Without effective pre-attack reconnaissance, an air commander will lack the information he needs to use his force to greatest effect. And unless he has prompt post-attack reconnaissance, he cannot determine whether or not an attack has been successful. Chapter 9, 'Reconnaissance to Berlin', illustrates the skills and the special kind of bravery needed to fly, alone, deep into enemy territory in an unarmed aircraft.

As has been said, the German 'Blitz' on Britain in 1940 and 1941 was the first-ever large-scale night bombing campaign. Yet this campaign was soon being dwarfed by that mounted by RAF night bombers against targets in Germany. Usually the cloak of darkness shielded the bombers from the ferocity of the German night fighter and gun defences, but on 30/31 March 1944 events conspired to strip away that safeguard. The resultant action is described in Chapter 10, 'The Nuremberg Disaster'.

By the spring of 1944 the US heavy bombers had protection from strong forces of escorting fighters all the way to and from their targets. The cumulative effect of these attacks was the devastation of major parts of the German war economy and in particular the synthetic oil industry. *Reich* Air Defence fighter units found themselves locked into a losing battle of attrition against the American fighters, in which they suffered heavy losses in aircraft and pilots. The history of warfare provides many examples of actions where a few courageous men overcame a numerically superior foe. The *Luftwaffe* sought such an outcome when it introduced the novel attack methods described in Chapter 11, 'Day of the Sturmgruppe'.

The appearance of the Messerschmitt Me 262 jet fighter in action in the autumn of 1944 brought a huge advance in combat performance and firepower compared with anything that had gone before. These are important attributes for a fighter aircraft, but they are not, by themselves, sufficient to bring about the defeat of a well-resourced and well-trained foe. Chapter 12, 'The Jets get their Chance', reviews the problems of bringing the revolutionary Messerschmitt 262 fighter into action in sufficient numbers.

During the late 1930s the accepted wisdom of the time was that manoeuvring combat between fighters was a thing of the past. The RAF *Manual of Air Tactics*, 1938 Edition, solemnly stated that 'Manoeuvre at high speeds in air fighting is not now practicable, because the effect of gravity on the human body causes a temporary loss of consciousness, deflecting shooting becomes difficult and accuracy is hard to obtain.' Apart from the first of those statements, the others were (and, indeed still are) true. The effect of gravity on the human body during high-speed manoeuvres *does* cause temporary loss of consciousness, deflection shooting *does* become difficult and as a result accuracy *is* hard to obtain. When the matter was subjected to the acid test of combat in the Second World War, however, it soon became clear that although deflection shooting was 'difficult' and accuracy was 'hard to obtain', these were not insurmountable obstacles. Although manoeuvring combat was difficult and tiring, with determination it was certainly possible.

Following the introduction of swept-wing jet fighters able to exceed the speed of sound in a dive, in the late 1940s, it was again fashionable to sound the death-knell of fighter-versus-fighter combat—until the Korean War taught people otherwise. The notion was resurrected a decade later with the emergence of Mach 2 fighters armed with air-to-air missiles—until the air war over North Vietnam laid that particular ghost to rest for all time. The largest dogfight of that period is described in Chapter 13, 'Furball over Hai Duong'.

The action over Hai Duong demonstrated that fighter pilots are sometimes forced to fight on terms quite different from those for which they had trained in peacetime. Another example of this occurred during the Falklands Conflict in 1982, when Sea Harrier pilots defended the amphibious landing operation at San Carlos against attacks by the far larger Argentine Air Force and Navy. Chapter 14 'Low Level Drama in front of San Carlos', describes the heaviest day of air fighting during that conflict.

Air transport is yet another aspect of air warfare that is possible only if one's opponent does not possess air superiority over the operating area. In Chapter 15, 'The Epic of "Bravo November"', the Falklands War provides an example of how a single large helicopter, handled with skill and resolution, had a considerable effect on a land campaign.

The Vietnam War spawned two families of air-to-ground weapons that have brought unprecedented accuracy to attacks on land targets: the laser-guided bomb and the electro-optically guided bomb. During the final years of 'The Cold War', the US 48th Tactical Fighter Wing equipped with F-111Fs perfected the techniques for delivering these weapons. Chapter 15, 'Precision Attack—By Night', describes the unit's operations during the recent conflict in the Persian Gulf area.

At any time the act of being shot down is a traumatic experience, as an aircraft suddenly becomes incapable of sustained flight. Chapter 16, 'St Valentine's Day Shoot-Down', describes an example that occurred during one of the recent attacks on Iraq.

This series of accounts is intended to provide the reader with a wide-ranging overview of the business of aerial warfare. Some of the impressions gained may not fit easily into the reader's pre-conceived framework of ideas on this complex subject. It is not my intention to be deliberately controversial, but neither have I repeated some of the comforting and comfortable assertions of 'established wisdom' that I consider to be invalid. By setting out the facts in this way, I trust that readers will be able to take a more critical line with the material that appears before them in future.

Author's Note
Unless stated otherwise, in this account all miles are statute miles and all speeds are given in statute miles per hour. Gallons and tons are given in Imperial measurements. Times are given in local time for the area where the incident described took place. Weapon calibres are given in the units normal for the weapon being described, e.g. Oerlikon 20mm cannon or Browning .5in machine gun. Where an aircraft's offensive armament load is stated, this is the normal load carried by that type of aircraft during operations and not the larger maximum figure stated in makers' brochures and reproduced in most aircraft data books.

Acknowledgment
I thank my friend Martin Middlebrook for kind permission to use first-person quotations from his books *The Schweinfurt-Regensburg Mission* and *The Nuremberg Raid*, in Chapters 8 and 10 respectively.

Alfred Price
Uppingham, Rutland
January 1993

CHAPTER ONE

Above the Fields of France

The story of No 84 Squadron Royal Flying Corps, which was sent into action over France in the autumn of 1917, and of its commander Major W. Sholto Douglas, who became one of the leading air combat tacticians of his time.

AIR-TO-AIR COMBAT had its origins over the Western Front during the First World War, after reconnaissance planes started to carry machine guns so that they could engage their enemy counterparts if they chanced to meet them. Then in the summer of 1915 the German Air Service introduced the Fokker monoplane, the first aircraft to be an effective destroyer of its own kind. A single-seater, the Fokker had a performance that no two-seater of the time could match. More importantly, its machine gun fired forwards through the propeller disc and had an interrupter system to prevent rounds striking the propeller blades. The deployment of the Fokker monoplane in small numbers enabled German pilots to seize air superiority, but the effect proved transitory as its features were soon copied by the enemy.

From then on each side strove to wrest air superiority from its opponent, or hold on to it. This led to the accelerated development of all aspects of aviation and in particular that of the fighter aircraft. The warring sides fielded a succession of new types that, with ever more powerful engines, could fly faster and higher and climb faster. Structures became heavier and a lot stronger and aeroplanes' armaments became more lethal.

As the fighter aircraft became more effective, talented individuals began to amass sizeable victory scores and establish their names as exponents of the new form of warfare: Germans like Max Immelmann, Oswald Boelke and Manfred von Richthofen, Frenchmen like Georges Guynemer, Charles Nungesser and René Fonck and from Britain men like 'Mick' Mannock, Albert Ball and James McCudden. Every country needs to have heroes in time of war, and almost overnight the ace pilots became national celebrities.

Yet although these men were prepared to fight each other to the death and on rare occasions did so, they had much in common. Invariably they were gifted with excellent eyesight, which allowed them to see their enemy at great distances and usually before they themselves were seen. They had learned to use the sun or cloud cover to approach an enemy unseen, and they could size up the tactical situation at a glance and assess the quickest way to reach a firing position on their foe. Some of them were exceptionally fine shots, while others compensated for a lack of this ability by closing to short range to deliver their lethal burst. Most of their victims were taken by surprise and never saw their assailant before their aircraft was hit. Contrary to popular belief, the high-scoring aces scored relatively few victories in one-versus-one turning combats, or during the swirling dogfights. Those who survived long enough to reach that status knew that the risks incurred in this type of fighting were too great and the chances of success too small. By the end of 1917 the day of the lone aerial hunter—the man who went out alone to stalk enemy planes—was nearing its end. Few could operate effectively in this way, and the pilots of average ability achieved much more if they flew as part of a well-led unit than if they were left to their own devices. Air fighting had become a team affair and, as in a football match, the well-led team would usually defeat the bunch of talented but undisciplined individualists.

* * *

Born in 1893, William Sholto Douglas joined the Royal Flying Corps in 1914. Early the following year he flew his first operational flights with No 2 Squadron. In April 1916 he commanded No 43 Squadron equipped with Sopwith 1½ Strutters and led the unit in action. In August 1917 Douglas took command of No 84 Squadron, then in the process of forming at Lilibourne near Rugby with eight-een S.E.5A fighters. Of the 24 pilots assigned to the unit, only Douglas and his three flight commanders had previous air fighting experience.

In September No 84 Squadron moved to Liettres in northern France, ten miles behind the front line, and underwent a short period of preparation for combat. Its first mission over enemy territory took place on 15 October, when it escorted six de Havilland 4 bombers attacking an ammunition dump. During a tussle with enemy fighters Lieutenant Edmund Krohn claimed the destruction of an Albatros fighter, the unit's first victory. But any elation that might have been felt was tempered by the loss of Lieutenant Lord, who was shot down and taken prisoner.

Although the S.E.5A had the edge in performance over the Albatros D V, the main German type it met in action, the Squadron suffered painful losses during its initiation into combat. At the time the Battle of Passchendaele was in full swing, and the unit was in action on almost every day and suffered severe losses. During a particularly hard-fought action on 31 October, for example, Captain Leask lead a six-aircraft flight down to attack four hostile aircraft seen below them. Then a dozen Albatros fighters pounced from above and the would-be hunters became the prey. Two S.E.5As were shot down and their pilots killed, while the Squadron claimed the destruction of two enemy aircraft.

During its first sixteen days in action, No 84 Squadron lost nine pilots killed or taken prisoner, more than one-third of its complement. Its total claim over the period amounted to five enemy aircraft. On this inauspicious start Douglas later reflected:

It was a hard school for a new and untried Squadron and at first, owing to the inexperience of the pilots, we suffered casualties. But bitter experience is a quick teacher . . .

In November the Battle of Passchendaele petered out and the ground fighting slackened. This, coupled with a general deterioration in the weather, led to a marked reduction in air activity. Replacements arrived to fill the gaps in the ranks, and those pilots that had survived the harsh initial baptism of fire emerged with a better grasp of the realities of air combat. Now the unit was allowed a breathing space to consider past mistakes and build on its hard-won fighting experience. After a couple of moves it ended the year based at Flez near St Quentin.

Douglas soon revealed himself as a shrewd tactician and a perceptive commander. Although his own victory score would never be impressive, he produced a workable set of tactics and ensured that his pilots complied with them. The lessons of the bloody initiation into combat were well learned and No 84 Squadron evolved into an effective force, confident in its abilities and with a high ratio of victories to losses.

After the war Douglas wrote a long report on his experiences as a fighter commander, in which he set down the techniques that led to success in air combat and those that did not. He quickly grasped the fundamental lesson that has been part of the combat philosophy of every successful fighter pilot, before or since:

> A lesson that we soon learnt was that there are occasions when it is wrong to accept battle, that one must always strive to take the enemy at a disadvantage. Equally, one must not be taken at a disadvantage oneself and this often entails a deliberate refusal of battle and a retirement so that the enemy's advantage may be nullified. If for instance that advantage is height, then one should retreat, climb hard, and go back and seek out the enemy at his own height or higher. Of course there are occasions when battle has to be accepted at a disadvantage—if, for instance, one sees another British squadron being overwhelmed by superior numbers, then obviously whatever the odds one must accept battle. But normally one should force the battle upon the enemy, not have the battle forced on oneself.

Douglas appreciated the strengths and weaknesses of the S.E.5A, compared with the enemy types that his unit met in action. As well as its excellent speed, climbing and diving performance compared its opponents, the S.E.5A had other useful attributes. It was a rugged aircraft that would accept a lot of mishandling, and the commander felt that that was particularly important:

> The S.E. was strong in design and construction, and it did not break up in the air when roughly handled as certain other types were apt to do. *Nothing undermines a pilot's confidence in his machine so much as doubts as to its strength* [author's emphasis].

The pilot's view from the S.E.5A was better than from most other contemporary biplane fighter types—an important characteristic in an air action where the side that was the first to detect its opponent possessed the initiative in any combat that followed. The aircraft was also a stable firing platform, particularly in the dive, and this was another factor that Douglas considered useful:

> It was very steady when diving fast; the pilot could therefore take very careful aim when diving to attack (and nine times out of ten he attacks by diving). This is an

advantage pertaining to all stable machines—the faster one dives, the steadier becomes one's gun platform. An unstable machine like a Camel or a Sopwith Dolphin is apt to 'hunt' when diving at high speeds, i.e. to vary its angle of dive from time to time in spite of the pilot's best endeavours to prevent it . . . Good shooting under these circumstances is rendered very difficult.

If an S.E.5A pilot were forced on to the defensive in combat, a steep dive would enable him to pick up speed quickly and draw away from his opponent, even one that was faster in straight and level flight. It was a useful method of breaking out of an action if a pilot was hard-pressed, if his guns had jammed or if he had run out of ammunition.

The S.E.5A was less manoeuvrable than many contemporary fighter types, though Douglas played down the importance of this attribute in combat:

The S.E. has often been criticised as being heavy on the controls for a single-seater, and so insufficiently manoeuvrable. In the days when aerial fighting was a series of combats between individuals, it is true that the manoeuvrability of the individual machine was all-important. In 1918, however, it was no longer the individual pilot but the flight flying in close formation that was the fighting unit; and the distinction will, I think, become more and more pronounced in future wars. In the present development of aerial fighting it is *the flight that fights as one unit* [author's emphasis]. Therefore it is the manoeuvrability of the flight that counts, not the manoeuvrability of the individual machine. If then a machine is sufficiently handy (as was the S.E.) to keep its place in the formation in any flight manoeuvre, it is of minor importance whether that machine is individually of a high degree of manoeuvrability or not.

It was found that supremely quick manoeuvring was nearly always a defensive measure; when attacked the pilot escaped the immediate consequences by swift manoeuvre. The attack on the other hand was usually delivered by a flight formation diving at high speed, so that in attack it was the manoeuvrability of the flight that counted. Now if you have a machine superior in performance to the enemy (as was the S.E. till the autumn of 1918), and your patrols are well led, you should very rarely be attacked or thrown on the defensive. Instead, you should be able so to manoeuvre your formation that, by virtue of your superior speed and climb, you yourself are always the attacker; which leads us to the conclusion that if your machines are superior in performance to those of the enemy, manoeuvrability is a very secondary consideration.

By trial and error Douglas arrived at what he considered to be the optimum fighting unit: a five-aircraft formation flying in 'V', stepped up from front to rear. Lacking radio, the aircraft flew close to the leader to observe his hand signals. The leader could also communicate by manoeuvres, though there was only a small range of easily understood messages that could be passed in this way. For example, banking gently to one side then to the other meant 'Close up'; flying an undulating path meant 'Open out'; to signal his intention to turn, the leader banked twice in the required direction, then began turning; and 'Enemy in sight' was indicated by banking the aircraft steeply from side to side several times.

S.E.5A

Role: Single-seat fighter.

Power: One Wolseley Viper 8-cylinder, liquid-cooled engine developing 200hp at take-off (other types of engine were also fitted, but the Viper was standard on No 84 Squadron's aircraft from March 1918 to the end of the war).

Armament: One Vickers .303in machine gun synchronized to fire through the propeller disc; one Lewis .303in machine gun mounted on top of the upper wing, firing above the propeller disc. There was provision for carrying four 25lb bombs on racks under the fuselage.

Performance: Maximum speed 128mph at 6,500ft; climb to 10,000ft, 10min 50sec; climb to 15,000ft, 20min 50sec.

Normal operational take-off weight: 1,988lb (no bombs carried).

Dimensions: Span 26ft 7½in; length 20ft 11in; wing area (both wings) 245.8 sq ft.

Date of first production S.E.5A: May 1917.

Douglas ordered that flight leaders make all of the tactical decisions, and the other pilots in the flight had to concentrate on maintaining position in formation and following instructions. The technique of co-ordinated search, in which every pilot in the formation scans an area of sky keeping watch for the enemy, was unknown. Given the poor training and experience level of the average squadron pilot at the time, it would probably have been unworkable.

By this stage of the war the German fighter units usually flew in formations of a dozen or more. They rarely ventured over the land battle, preferring to engage the enemy over their own territory. Lieutenant-Colonel Holt, the commander of the 22nd Wing of which No 84 Squadron was part, sent multi-squadron formations over hostile territory in an attempt to force the German fighting patrols into action. Typically, such a formation comprised a squadron of Sopwith Camels at 15,000ft, one of S.E.5As 16,000ft and one of Bristol fighters at 18,000ft. The tactic was a complete failure. The force could be seen from several miles, and any German fighting patrol in its path quickly drew away to the east. When the formation turned for home, having punched at an empty sky, the enemy fighters harried it from the sides and flanks and attempted to pick off stragglers.

Douglas took part in a few of these fighter sweeps and was scathing in his criticism of them. In his view the squadron-size offensive patrol was much more successful as a means of engaging the enemy. That, he felt, was the largest force that could be led effectively into action by one man. He developed a technique of using three flights flying some distance apart but in concert, each with a set role. In a typical patrol of this type, 'A' Flight flew in the lead at 15,000ft and its commander was in charge of the entire formation. 'B' Flight, in support, maintained position about half a mile behind 'A' Flight and flew in echelon some 500ft above it. 'C' Flight, also in support, flew farther behind 'A', echeloned on the opposite side to 'B' Flight and at 18,000ft. Describing the tactical employment of this force, Douglas commented:

The duty of 'B' Flight is to follow closely and conform to the movements of 'A' Flight. It does not attack on its own initiative—the initiative lies absolutely in the hands of the squadron patrol leader, i.e. the leader of 'A' Flight. This somewhat rigid formalism was found to be necessary owing to the tendency of the following flights to be drawn away into subsidiary combats, leaving the squadron leader unsupported. If the latter attacks, 'B' Flight does one of two things: it either reinforces 'A' Flight, if the enemy is sufficiently numerous to make this worth while; or it flies directly over the top of 'A' Flight and affords protection to 'A' Flight against enemy machines attacking from above. The third flight ('C' Flight) is the covering force: it flies as high as possible, and some two or three miles behind and to the flank of 'A' Flight. The leader follows 'A' Flight at a distance, and has orders never to come down to assist 'A' and 'B' Flights except in great emergency. The mere fact that 'C' Flight is circling high up over the combat is usually sufficient to prevent any but a very strong enemy formation from attacking the two lower flights.

Douglas took the view that the well-led and disciplined flight formation was the most effective means of destroying enemy aircraft for minimum losses, and in action he set great store on maintaining flight cohesion:

It was soon discovered that, as soon as the flight lost formation and was split up, casualties occurred. Also, that it was not when attacked that the flight was so liable to break up, as when [it was] attacking. When attacked, pilots naturally hung together for mutual protection; but when an attack was begun, pilots were apt to break off in pursuit of the particular German machine that they had marked down as their prey, and were then set upon while so isolated, and overwhelmed by superior numbers.

After much debate and in spite of opposition from the individualists in the squadron, we finally made a strict order that *no pilot was on any account to leave the formation* [author's emphasis], even to take an apparently easy opportunity of shooting down an enemy machine. The initiative in any attack lay wholly with the flight leader: if he dived to the attack, the whole flight dived with him; when he zoomed away after the attack, even if he had failed to shoot down the enemy attacked, all pilots zoomed away with him still keeping formation. This was found to be the only way of keeping the formation together during a combat; otherwise the flight was split up at the first onset, each pilot breaking off in pursuit of a different enemy machine, and then being defeated in detail.

The natural consequence of this order was that it was usually the flight commander who actually shot down the enemy machine. But, being the most experienced pilot, he was the most capable of doing this quickly and effectively. In addition, with his flight behind him to act as a buffer against any attack from behind, he could afford to concentrate all his powers on the destruction of the enemy machine. There was no need for him to be peering over his shoulder all the time, anxious lest he himself be attacked. His aiming and shooting were therefore the more careful and deliberate.

Unless it were unavoidable, No 84 Squadron refused to engage in dogfights with enemy fighters. The First World War dogfight has been likened to 'a bar room brawl with guns'. Once the opposing forces were committed, their commanders had no control over the action, and that was reason enough for Douglas to order his pilots keep out of them. These disciplined fighting tactics proved highly effective, particularly on 3 April 1918 when the unit engaged a large force of enemy Pfalz and Albatros fighters over Pozières and claimed the destruction of six enemy aircraft without loss to itself. A few weeks later, on the 25th, No 84 Squadron had another successful action when it claimed the destruction of nine Pfalz and Albatros fighters for the loss of one S.E.5A.

From time to time the Squadron was ordered to provide close escort for bomber formations attacking targets in hostile territory. Douglas hated this type of operation, and likened a fighting squadron tied to a bomber formation to a boxer trying to fight with one hand tied behind his back. He continued:

> . . . a fighting squadron on escort duty cannot attack the enemy formations that it encounters because if it did so, the bombers, proceeding on their course, would soon be out of sight and would thus be left unprotected. All that the fighting squadron can do is to wait until the enemy attacks and then to parry the blow. Moreover a bombing formation, if composed of machines with a good performance, of pilots who can fly in close formation and of observers who can shoot straight, can fight a very successful defensive action against even superior numbers.

In the decades to follow, fighter unit leaders of almost every nation would reiterate Douglas's sentiments.

The effectiveness of No 84 Squadron's tactics was quickly reflected in its ratio of victory claims to losses. During the four months from the beginning of December 1917 the unit claimed 68 enemy aircraft destroyed or sent out of control. Like most victory totals amassed during the conflict, it was almost certainly an overclaim, but, whatever the true figure, it was achieved for a loss of only two pilots killed in action, two taken prisoner and one wounded.

On 1 April 1918 the Royal Flying Corps was incorporated into the new Royal Air Force. At the time No 84 Squadron was too busily engaged in the fighting to notice anything different. It would take several months for the changes to filter through the command system, and business continued exactly as before.

ALBATROS D V
(The German fighter type most frequently encountered by No 84 Squadron, up to the spring of 1918)

Role: Single-seat fighter.
Power: One Mercedes D III 6-cylinder, liquid-cooled engine developing 160hp at take-off.
Armament: Two Spandau 7.9mm machine guns synchronized to fire through the propeller disc.
Performance: Maximum speed 102mph at 9,840ft; climb to 9,840ft, 17min 9sec.
Normal operational take-off weight: 2,018lb.
Dimensions: Span 29ft 8½in; length 24ft; wing area (both wings) 220.1 sq ft.
Date of first production Albatros D V: May 1917.

As has been said, Douglas himself did not achieve an impressive victory score. But several of his pilots did, notably Lieutenant Andrew Beauchamp Proctor. A diminutive South African only 5ft 1in tall, 'Procky' was so small that his aircraft was fitted with blocks on the rudder pedals so that he could reach them. His contemporaries described him as being extremely aggressive in the air, he had exceptionally keen vision and he was an excellent shot. Although a novice pilot when the unit first went into action, by the end of March 1918 he was a flight leader. By the following month, when he was promoted to Captain, his victory score stood at 5½ enemy aircraft.

During the final three months of the war No 84 Squadron became adept in the specialized technique of destroying enemy observation balloons. By this stage of the war the numerous Allied patrols over the battle front made life extremely hazardous for German planes on gunfire spotting missions. As a result, the German artillerymen came to rely on balloon-borne observers to direct fire against ground targets beyond the front line. If these balloons could be destroyed or kept on the ground, the effectiveness of the German artillery was much reduced and the life of the long-suffering British infantrymen was made much easier—hence the importance given to attacking these sausage-shaped targets.

Since they were filled with potentially explosive hydrogen gas and carried no defensive weapons, it might seem that the balloons were easy prey. As many a fighter pilot discovered to his cost, however, this was not the case. Hydrogen in an enclosed container—such as a balloon envelope—is not inflammable: like petrol, it becomes explosive only when it is mixed with oxygen in the correct ratio. To set the balloon on fire it was first necessary to puncture the envelope to allow the gas to escape and mix with the surrounding air, then ignite the mixture with tracer rounds. That meant that the rounds had to be concentrated on a particular part of the balloon, and attacks had to be pressed to within 50yds to achieve success. If there were rain, or if the air were moist, it was almost impossible to ignite a balloon.

Normally the German observation balloons flew at altitudes of between 1,500 and 4,500ft and had machine guns positioned around them to deter fighter attacks. If he saw enemy fighters approaching, the observer jumped from his basket by parachute and the balloon was winched down as rapidly as possible. Because the balloons flew at a relatively low altitude, anyone attacking one was himself liable to be attacked from above by enemy fighters. Douglas therefore devised a setpiece method of attacking the balloons, a variation of the tactics which had proved successful during the Squadron's offensive patrols. The Squadron crossed the front line in formation at altitudes around 10,000ft, as if flying an ordinary patrol. When the force reached a point above the balloons, the flight designated to attack them dived away. The pilots fanned out and each singled out a balloon to engage. One covering flight descended to 5,000ft to protect the attackers from enemy fighters, while the other flight stayed at 10,000ft to deter enemy planes going down to engage those below. During an attack on balloons, speed and surprise were essential.

Douglas noted:

It was . . . found to be best to dive steeply to a point about half a mile from the balloon and on a level with it; then to flatten out and go straight at the balloon with all the added velocity gained in the dive. At 200 yards' range one took a sighting shot with the Vickers and at fifty yards opened fire with the Lewis gun. One carried straight on to within about twenty yards of the balloon, firing all the time, hopped over it and zoomed away.

These attacks were invariably brisk affairs, with no more than ten minutes from the time the formation first crossed the front line until the last aircraft was back over friendly territory. The tactics were used successfully on several occasions and at the end of the war the Squadron's score stood at 50 balloons destroyed. On its best day for balloon attacks, 24 September 1918, the unit was in action twice. In the morning Beauchamp Proctor led an attack on a line of balloons: he shot down one and his colleagues shot down two more. That afternoon Captain Carl Falkenburg led a similar attack on a line of six balloons which resulted in the destruction of four. On both occasions the covering flights prevented enemy fighter patrols from interfering with the operations. In his report, Falkenburg noted that the attack

. . . took the enemy by surprise and we had four balloons in flames before he began to retaliate from the ground. By the time the Ack Ack and machine gun fire got really intense we were back in the clouds and succeeded in getting home almost unscathed. The top flight, led by Lt Nel, kept a good watch and kept just over us while we were attacking the balloons. They then escorted us home.

In the afternoon of 8 October Beauchamp Proctor engaged a Rumpler reconnaissance aircraft near Maretz and followed it down to low altitude to finish it off. His S.E.5A came under fire from the ground and he was hit in the arm. Nevertheless, he continued with the mission and made an unsuccessful attack on a balloon before returning to base. The wound proved more serious than initially thought, however, and he spent most of the next five months in hospital. By then his victory score stood at 54 enemy aircraft, including 16 observation balloons. Following a strong recommendation from Douglas, supported by corroborating statements by four other pilots, Beauchamp Proctor was awarded the Victoria Cross in recognition of his bravery and determination in combat.

* * *

Following their bloody initiation into combat, during which nine pilots were lost in less than three weeks, Douglas and the other survivors learned their craft quickly. During the twelve-month period from the early part of November 1917 until the Armistice exactly a year later, No 84 Squadron was continually in action and it took part in some of the heaviest fighting. The unit was credited with the destruction of 306 enemy aircraft, including 50 balloons. In the absence of effective verification procedures, it would be surprising if these claims were accurate; but, even if only half were true, the unit's score was still remarkable.

Many units achieved high victory scores by employing high-risk tactics and incurring heavy losses in the process. That was not Douglas's way. No 84 Squadron operated as a disciplined unit employing comparatively low-risk tactics, and that was reflected in the relatively low losses suffered in action—25 pilots killed, two taken prisoner and eighteen wounded. Few units engaged in prolonged heavy fighting over the Western Front got off so lightly.

After the war Douglas gained rapid promotion in the RAF and at the beginning of the Second World War he was Assistant Chief of Air Staff with the rank of Air Vice-Marshal. In the autumn of 1940 he was appointed to lead Fighter Command in succession to Sir Hugh Dowding. Later he became Commander-in-Chief RAF Middle East, and at the end of the war he was Commander-in-Chief Coastal Command. In 1948 he retired as Marshal of the Royal Air Force and soon afterwards, as Lord Douglas of Kirtleside, joined the board of the British Overseas Airways Corporation and played an important part in the development of that airline. He died in 1969.

CHAPTER TWO

The Rise and Demise of the Stuka

With its angular outline and screaming siren, the steep-diving Junkers
Ju 87 'Stuka' has come to epitomize the fast-moving, hard-hitting
Blitzkrieg tactics employed with such success by German armed forces
during the early part of the Second World War. In this chapter we examine
the ingredients of the aircraft's success, and the countermeasures that
brought about its defeat.

UNTIL THE ADVENT of guided weapons, the steep dive-attack was the most accurate method to deliver bombs on a defended target. Against small targets, bombing accuracy is a matter of paramount importance. A 1,000lb bomb missing the hard target by a few tens of yards will cause it no serious damage. It can be shown mathematically (though the author will resist the temptation) that if a bomb's miss distance is halved, its destructive effect is four times as great. If the miss distance is reduced by three-quarters, the destructive effect is increased *sixteen-fold*. Or, to put it another way, the same destructive effect can be achieved using *one-sixteenth* the weight of bombs. Those figures explain the rationale for the Stuka and its concept of operation: that a small weight of high explosive positioned accurately will be much more effective than a considerably greater amount of explosive positioned less accurately. (Today, this argument justifies the greater cost and complication, but the far greater accuracy, of the 'smart' weapons.)

* * *

The word 'Stuka' is a contraction of the German word *Sturzkampfflugzeug* meaning 'dive-bomber'. Strictly speaking, the term refers to all aircraft capable of performing that role and not merely to a particular type. Yet by common usage over many years, 'Junkers 87' and 'Stuka' have come to be synonymous, and they will be treated as such in this account.

The Junkers Ju 87 was designed without compromise as a steep-diving bomber, and everything else was subordinated to that requirement. The 'Berta', the main production version until early in 1941 and the one that established the type's reputation, carried a 1,100lb bomb load. The fixed, spatted undercarriage gave the aircraft a decidedly dated look, and in horizontal flight its maximum speed was only 238mph. Yet during a diving attack the drag from the fixed under-carriage was a positive asset, when combined with that from the dive brakes extended under the wings: slowed by these protuberances, the Ju 87 was inherently stable in its near-vertical attack dive. With the engine throttled back, the machine reached a terminal velocity of only about 350mph (a cleaner aircraft would have attained a greater terminal velocity in the dive; that meant that the pilot had to dive less steeply or release the bombs and begin the pull-out at a higher altitude, and either factor would have reduced bombing accuracy).

Once the bombs had been released, a specially designed mechanism initiated a firm but smooth 6g pull-out from the dive. The Ju 87's rugged structure was designed to withstand this manoeuvre with a safety margin in case—as sometimes happened—the bombs failed to leave the aircraft. It was an important consideration: during a 6g pull-out, 1,100 pounds of bombs still in place added more than 3 tons to the load the aircraft's structure had to support.

Just as the requirements of the steep-diving attack dominated the design of the Ju 87, so they dictated the tactics of using the aircraft in action. The description that follows covers a typical 'set piece' dive-bombing attack by these aircraft.

On their way to the target the Ju 87s usually flew at about 11,000ft, the highest altitude at which crews could go safely without resorting to oxygen. The aircraft flew in three-plane 'vics' and, depending on the size and importance of the target, a *Staffel* (up to nine aircraft) or *Gruppe* (up to 30 aircraft) formation flew with the vics in line astern with an interval of 300yds between each.

For an accurate attack, it was important that the aircraft were heading directly into the wind when they commenced their dives. As he neared the target, the formation leader kept an eye open for smoke rising from the ground, to determine the wind direction, and aligned the attack run accordingly. Immediately before he commenced his dive, each Ju 87 pilot re-trimmed the aircraft for the dive and set the briefed bomb-release altitude (above sea level) on the contacting altimeter.

Inset into the floor of the cockpit in front of the pilot's seat was a window, through which he could see the target as it slid into position beneath the aircraft. A few seconds before commencing the dive, he throttled back the engine to idling and operated a lever to rotate the dive brakes to the maximum-drag position. The dive brakes produced a severe nose-up trim change to the aircraft, and to compensate for it a trim tab fitted to the elevators was lowered automatically.

When the formation leader commenced his dive, the rest of the aircraft in the formation followed in turn. For attacks on targets of small horizontal extent, for example bridges or small buildings, the Ju 87s usually approached in echelon formation, peeled into the dive and attacked in line astern. Against larger or better-defended targets, for example harbours or marshalling yards, the dive-bombers would usually bunt into their dives in three-aircraft vics and attack together to split the defensive fire.

Once established in its 80-degree dive, the Ju 87 was a stable platform and it was easy for the pilot to position the target under his reflector sight and hold it there. Speed built up relatively slowly, and it took a dive through 8,000ft for the aircraft to reach its terminal velocity of 350mph. The dive lasted about 20 seconds, allowing plenty of time to line up on the target. The accuracy of the attack depended upon maintaining a constant dive angle, and to assist in this a protractor was etched into the perspex on each side of the cockpit canopy so that the pilot could read off his angle during the dive.

When the aircraft reached a point 2,000ft above the bomb-release altitude previously set on the contacting altimeter, a warning horn sounded in the cockpit. When the aircraft reached the previously set bomb-release altitude, typically 2,300ft above the ground, the warning horn ceased. That was the signal to release the bombs. It will be remembered that before commencing the dive, a trim tab fitted to the elevators was lowered automatically to compensate for the nose-up pitching moment caused when the dive brakes were placed in the high-drag position. Now, the operation of releasing the bombs also activated a powerful spring, which returned the elevator trim tab sharply to the neutral position. The nose of the aircraft pitched up sharply, pulling the aircraft firmly but smoothly out of the dive. In this pre-set manoeuvre, the lowest point reached was about 1,000ft above the target—enough to give a margin of safety from exploding bombs and enemy small-arms fire. As the nose of the aircraft rose above the horizon, the pilot returned the dive brakes in the low-drag position, opened the throttle, re-trimmed the aircraft and turned on to the pre-briefed escape heading.

On completion of their training, German dive-bomber pilots were expected to put half of their bombs within a circle 25m (27yds) in radius centred on the target. (For comparison, the aiming error from a horizontal bomber releasing its bombs from high altitude was about three times as great.) In combat the bombing was invariably less accurate, because of the lack of familiarity with the target and the distractions caused by the enemy defences. As a result, the average bombing errors in combat were two or three times those achieved on the training ranges. Nevertheless, against (say) a circular target with a radius of 80yds, with moderately heavy anti-aircraft gun defences, a nine-aircraft *Staffel* of Ju 87s stood a good chance of scoring direct hits with half the bombs. Against very small, hard targets such as tanks of the period (typical dimensions about 7yds long and 3yds wide), which could survive anything except a direct hit or a very near miss, the Stukas were relatively ineffective.

To sum up, by a combination of its near-vertical dive, relatively low diving speed and low bomb-release altitude, the Ju 87 was able to deliver (unguided) bombs with an accuracy not previously achieved in action and rarely attained since. During the Second World War other types of aircraft also carried out steep-diving attacks, but these released their bombs from altitudes somewhat higher than those of the Ju 87 and their accuracy was correspondingly reduced.

* * *

During the invasion of Poland, in September 1939, the Ju 87 established a formidable reputation in combat. These aircraft were used to deliver pin-point attacks on bridges, rail targets and troop concentrations well behind from the front line—what are now termed 'battlefield air interdiction' missions.

Attacks on airfields met with less success. During the period of tension preceding the invasion, the Polish Air Force re-deployed most of its combat flying units to well-camouflaged field landing grounds. As a result, few military planes were lost during the attacks on the larger airfields and most of them were not combat types. Yet, although the Polish Air Force survived much of the initial onslaught, it was too small and its equipment was too outdated to pose a serious threat to German air operations. The Polish forces were poorly equipped with anti-aircraft guns for the protection of targets and, operating with little hindrance, the Ju 87 units struck hard and with great accuracy.

Despite numerous accounts that have suggested otherwise, over Poland the Ju 87 units were rarely used for close air support operations, that is to say against targets within a few hundred yards of friendly ground forces. The Ju 87 could deliver an accurate steep-diving attack only against a target that was clearly visible from 10,000ft (or nearly two miles). Camouflaged troop positions in the battle area were difficult to see from such an altitude, and even more difficult to attack. Moreover, as the recent war in the Persian Gulf has shown, positive identification of troops in the battle area is a demanding business, and there is an ever-present risk that bombs might fall on the very troops they are supposed to assist.

The dive-bomber was a new and effective weapon and, above all, it was predominantly a *German* weapon. In those circumstances the German propaganda machine can hardly be blamed for playing the aircraft for all it was worth. Among friends and foes alike, the legend of the invincibility of the Stukas was established. Significantly, the number of Ju 87s in service at any time was never large. Over Poland, for example, the *Luftwaffe* committed every operational Ju 87 unit, but there were only about 370 aircraft.

On 10 May 1940 German forces launched their all-out *Blitzkrieg* campaign in the west, and from the first the Stukas were heavily committed. In one of many attacks flown by the dive-bombers that day, *Major* Walter Hagen led the 30 aircraft of *Trägergruppe 186* into the air from Hannweiler near Bad Kreuznach. (*Träger* = aircraft carrier; the unit was earmarked to operate from the aircraft carrier *Graf Zeppelin* when it was completed, but in the meantime it flew as a normal combat unit.)

The dive-bombers' objective was the major French Air Force base at Frescaty near Metz, some 70 miles away, and the attack was planned to take place at dawn. The aircraft took off and assembled into formation in the dark, each with a 550lb bomb under the fuselage and four 110-pounders on the underwing racks. The dive-bombers had no close escort, but a *Gruppe* of Messerschmitts was sweeping the route ahead of it to drive away any enemy planes that might be airborne. *Hauptmann* Helmut Mahlke described the action, from the time the Stukas arrived in the target area:

> In the turn we went into line astern, thirty Ju 87s following each other into the attack. As we lined up for our dives the flak opened up at us, but their shooting was slow and it did not bother us much. The target assigned to my *Kette* [vic] was the airship hangar, I could see it clearly. When it was my turn to attack, I banked my aircraft then pushed into an 80-degree dive. At 700m I released my bombs in a salvo, then began my pull-out. As I did so I looked at the hangar and at first it seemed that nothing had happened. Then the building expanded, rather like a toy balloon when somebody blows into it. Suddenly, the structure collapsed in a cloud of smoke and debris.

After delivering their attacks the Ju 87s reassembled into formation and headed for home, having suffered no losses.

During the next six weeks, Mahlke's unit was in operation on almost every day that the weather allowed, with crews flying as many as four missions a day. By the final week in May, Allied forces in northern France were being pushed relentlessly towards the coast, and Operation 'Dynamo' began to evacuate troops from Dunkirk and the beaches to the east. On 1 June Mahlke took part in an attack on the port and had his first encounter with an RAF fighter:

> It tried to shoot me down but almost certainly it ran out of ammunition before it could do so. The pilot curved around, moved into formation alongside me, saluted and pulled away for home. It was an act of chivalry that could never have happened in Russia . . .

After the Dunkirk evacuation ended, the German ground forces regrouped and moved against the French forces trying to re-establish a defensive line across northern France. The Stukas resumed operations in support of advancing German units, and during this phase there occurred an incident which impressed on Mahlke the risks of attacking targets in the vicinity of friendly forces. On 17 June he was ordered to lead his *Staffel* against a French troop position at Chatillon-sur-Seine near Dijon, in an area some distance ahead of German forces which threatened to hold up the advance. The approach flight was uneventful and Mahlke began his attack-dive, but then he noticed Very lights rising from the ground and men hastily laying out recognition panels. The area was in German hands! Mahlke pulled out of the dive and ordered his crews to abandon the attack. It was a close call: his unit had come close to bombing friendly troops in error. Later it transpired that French resistance in the area had collapsed and that the German advance had been much faster than expected.

During the campaign in the West, *Trägergruppe 186* flew about 1,500 sorties, in the course of which it lost fifteen crews out of its establishment of 40. The overall loss rate was about 1 per cent, not a high figure, but the cumulative loss during the six weeks of hard fighting amounted to 40 per cent of the air crew. At that stage of the war the war losses in crews and aircraft were made good almost immediately from the replacement units, but it was an uncomfortable pointer to the problems that would arise during a lengthy campaign.

The Battle of Britain opened in July 1940, and the large-scale bombardment of targets on the British mainland began on 12 August. That day there were attacks by Stukas on the radar stations at Pevensey, Rye, Dover, Dunkirk (in Kent) and Ventnor. The radars proved difficult targets, however. They were small objectives and their vital parts were protected by blast walls. Although the openwork metal towers supporting the radar aerials might appear fragile, they presented only a small area to blast pressure or bomb splinters and it required almost a direct hit to knock one down. Although most of the radar stations suffered damage, following hasty repairs all except one was back in operation on the following day.

The largest co-ordinated attack ever mounted by Stukas took place on 18 August 1940, 'The Hardest Day'. One hundred and nine Ju 87s drawn from *Sturz-*

kampfgeschwader 3 and *77*, escorted by more than 150 Messerschmitt Bf 109 fighters, set out to attack the airfields at Gosport, Ford and Thorney Island and the radar station at Poling. British radars observed the approaching attack force in good time, and the fighter controllers scrambled 68 Spitfires and Hurricanes to meet it. The defenders were still climbing into position to intercept when the Stuka formations crossed the coast and prepared to begin their attack-dives. The escorting Messerschmitts with each dive-bomber *Gruppe* now split into two parts, one remaining with the dive-bombers at high altitude while the other descended to 3,000ft ready to protect the Ju 87s when they pulled out of the dives and were at their most vulnerable.

At that moment, when the high-level escort was at its weakest, eighteen Hurricanes of Nos 43 and 601 Squadrons bounded into the Ju 87s of *I Gruppe* of *Sturzkampfgeschwader 77* as they were about to commence their attack on the airfield at Thorney Island. *Oberleutnant* Johannes Wilhelm, piloting one of the Stukas, heard the radio warning of the approaching fighters as he prepared to begin his dive. Behind him, *Unteroffizier* Anton Woerner, his rear gunner, squinted into the bright sun, looking for the enemy. Then, appearing as if from nowhere and with guns belching fire, the Hurricanes charged into the German formation. Wilhelm glimpsed three or four British fighters roar past him in rapid succession. To one side of him a Stuka burst into flames and slid out of the formation. Then Wilhelm felt his aircraft shudder and engine oil streamed back over his cabin. Then the cockpit began to fill with smoke: the aircraft was on fire! Wilhelm rolled the dive-bomber on to its back and shouted '*Raus!*' ('Get out!'). Both men slid back their canopies, released their straps and tumbled clear of the stricken dive-bomber.

As the Stukas commenced their attack-dives, individual Hurricanes followed them down, loosing off bursts whenever they could bring their sights to bear. Contrary to what some accounts have suggested, however, a Ju 87 in the dive was *almost invulnerable* to fighter attack. Flight Lieutenant Frank Carey of No 43 Squadron, who led the Hurricane attack that day, commented:

> In the dive they were very difficult to hit, because in a fighter one's speed built up so rapidly that one went screaming past him. But he couldn't dive for ever . . .

Oberleutnant Otto Schmidt released his bombs on Thorney Island and the Stuka was pulling itself out of the dive when something behind him caught his eye—an enemy fighter, looming large. His rear gunner was not firing back, and suddenly he realized why not—the unfortunate man was collapsed lifeless in his seat. In concentrating on making an accurate attack, Schmidt had failed to notice that his own aircraft had been hit. He pushed the Stuka into a side-slip to reduce speed and the British fighter shot past.

As the dive-bombers pulled away from their targets at low altitude, the leading Ju 87s flew at low speed to allow those behind could catch up easily. The aircraft flew in a loose gaggle, and if one came under attack from an enemy fighter it accelerated and flew past one or more of the others. If the fighter attempted to follow, it had to expose itself to fire from other Ju 87s in the gaggle. In the past the

---

JUNKERS JU 87B-1

Role: Two-seat dive-bomber.

Power: One Junkers Jumo 211 Da 12-cylinder, liquid-cooled engine developing 1,200hp at take-off.

Armament: Normal bomb load one 550lb bomb under the fuselage and four 110lb bombs under the wings; two Rheinmetall Borsig MG 17 7.9mm machine guns in the wings; one Rheinmetall Borsig MG 15 7.9mm machine gun in a flexible mounting firing rearwards.

Performance: (Without bomb load) Maximum speed 238mph at 13,130ft; maximum cruising speed 209mph at 12,145ft; maximum range 490 miles; service ceiling 26,240ft.

Normal operational take-off weight: 9,560lb.

Dimensions: Span 45ft 3¼in; length 36ft 1in; wing area 343 sq ft.

Date type entered production: May 1938

---

tactic had sometimes been effective in forcing fighters to break off the chase, but now several British squadrons were piling into the fight. The 25-mile strip of coastline between Bognor and Gosport became a turmoil of over 300 aircraft twisting and turning to bring guns to bear, or to avoid guns being brought to bear.

Running over the Isle of Wight from the west, Flight Lieutenant Derek Boitel-Gill, at the head of eleven Spitfires of No 152 Squadron, caught sight of the mêlée below. He ordered the unit into line astern and dived into the thick of the fighting. He closed on one of the dive-bombers, fired a four-second burst and saw the enemy go straight into the sea. Pilot Officer Eric Marrs followed his leader and later wrote:

> We dived after them and they went down to 100 feet above the water. Then followed a running chase out to sea. The evasive action they took was to throttle back and do steep turns to right and left, so that we would not be able to follow them and would overshoot. There were, however, so many of them that if one was shaken off the tail of one there was always another to sit on.

Marrs fired at several of the dive-bombers and saw one of them strike the sea, streaming burning petrol from its port wing. He continued his attacks until he ran out of ammunition.

The Stukas hit their targets with great precision, scarcely a single bomb falling outside the immediate area surrounding each target. Ford airfield was put out of action for several weeks, while those at Thorney Island and Gosport continued in use though at reduced efficiency. Twenty-one aircraft were wrecked on the ground. The radar station at Poling suffered severe damage, though following repairs it was back in use after a few days.

Of the Stuka *Gruppen* involved, one, *I* of *Sturzkampfgeschwader 77*, was hit particularly hard: of the 28 Stukas taking part in the attack, ten were shot down, one was damaged beyond repair and four returned with serious damage. More than half the unit's aircraft had been destroyed or damaged. The unit's commander, *Hauptmann* Herbert Meisel, was among those killed. The other three

Gruppen lost only six aircraft shot down and two damaged. Considering the force as a whole, 21 per cent of aircraft had been destroyed or damaged—too great a loss to be accepted as a matter of course.

The action on 18 August 1940 was the first real setback suffered by the Stukas, and it served to highlight a weakness that would be demonstrated again and again as the war progressed: the aircraft was a fine offensive weapon, but only if it could operate without hinderance from enemy fighters. If air superiority had not been secured, the dive-bomber units could expect heavy losses.

The Stukas next went into action over the Mediterranean after 150 of these aircraft were deployed to Sicily to support the Italian bombardment of Malta and the convoys taking supplies to the beleaguered island. On 10 January 1941 the Ju 87 revealed its devastating effectiveness against capital ships of the Royal Navy. In attacks on ships manoeuvring in open water, dive-bombing was far more effective than horizontal bombing. A dive-bomber pilot could follow the ship during its evasive turn, re-aligning his sight to aim at a point in the sea immediately in front of the vessel. The time of flight of the bombs after release, about five seconds, was too short for any subsequent change of helm to take effect.

That day the target was a battle group comprising the aircraft carrier *Illustrious*, two battleships and eight destroyers escorting a convoy of supply ships bound for Malta and Greece. The striking force comprised 43 Ju 87s, drawn from *I Gruppe* of *Sturzkampfgeschwader 1* and *II Gruppe* of *StG 2*. At the time the German aircraft were first detected on radar approaching the force, the four Fulmar fighters airborne were at low altitude and nearly out of ammunition, having driven off an attack by Italian torpedo bombers. The carrier turned into wind and launched four more fighters, but it was too late for them to climb to meet the raiders before the attack began. The Ju 87s began their dives without interference from enemy fighters, concentrating on *Illustrious* as their main target. Admiral Cunningham, the Royal Navy force commander, later wrote of their attack:

> There was no doubt we were watching complete experts. We could not but admire the skill and precision of it all. The attacks were pressed home to point blank range, and as they pulled out of their dives, some of them were seen to fly along the flight deck of *Illustrious* below the level of her funnel.

From start to finish the action took only seven minutes, by the end of which the carrier had suffered seven direct hits and one near-miss:

Bomb No 1 hit and destroyed the starboard S.2 pom-pom (anti-aircraft gun) and killed most of the crew.

Bomb No 2 perforated the forward end of the flight deck and passed overboard, exploding 10ft above the waterline. This caused extensive splinter damage to compartments near the waterline and started a fire in one of them.

Bomb No 3 exploded in the after lift well about 10–20ft below the flight deck, causing severe damage to the lift structure and electrical equipment and wrecking a Fulmar fighter on the lift.

Bomb No 4 perforated the armoured flight deck and exploded just above the hangar deck. This caused serious damage to the forward lift and the surrounding hangar deck structure. The blast blew away the fire curtains, causing numerous casualties, and started a serious fire in the hangar. Several aircraft in the hangar were destroyed.

Bomb No 5 hit the after end of the after lift, adding to the damage caused by bomb No 3.

Bomb No 6 perforated a pom-pom gun platform, passed through the ship and went overboard without detonating. A fire was started in two mess decks.

Bomb No 7 hit the after lift well and this completed the destruction of the lift structure.

Bomb No 8 was a near-miss off the starboard side which caused minor damage to the structure and slight flooding.

To add to the damage, a shot-down Ju 87 crashed into the carrier's flight deck near the after lift well, starting a further fire in that much-battered area.

The onslaught left the Royal Navy's newest aircraft carrier in dire distress, with fires blazing out of control below her decks and tongues of flame shooting from the after lift well. The rudders were out of action and she headed for Malta, steered by using differential revolutions on the main engines. The ship could no longer operate her aircraft, and those that were airborne were ordered to fly to Malta.

A follow-up attack during the late afternoon by fifteen Ju 87s caused a further direct hit near the after lift, adding to the damage to that area, and two near-misses close to the stern. That evening, with the fires inside the hull still burning out of control, the pummelled carrier reached Malta and tied up in Valetta harbour. During the attacks 83 of her crew had been killed and 100 wounded.

While *Illustrious* was undergoing repairs in Valetta, she was subjected to further attacks. Yet another direct hit near the after lift caused further damage to that part of the ship. Near-misses caused damage to machinery in the boiler room. Despite these intrusions, essential repairs were completed in a remarkably short time. After dark on 23 January, unnoticed by the enemy, the carrier limped out from Malta and headed for Alexandria. More than a year would elapse before she was again ready for operations. The action established that the waters within range of the Stuka bases in Sicily were now virtually off-limits to Royal Navy capital ships.

The Ju 87s would achieve further destruction against the Royal Navy during the invasion of Crete in May 1941 and the subsequent evacuation of Allied forces. And they would demonstrate their effectiveness yet again when German forces invaded the Soviet Union in the following month. Yet the heyday of the Stuka was fast drawing to a close. From the beginning of 1942 each of Germany's enemies appreciated the potent threat posed by the Ju 87s when they could operate without restriction, and the vital need to contain that threat. The best answer, of course, was to have enough fighters to make attacks by the dive-bombers too expensive to contemplate. That requirement had been easy to assert but difficult to fulfil, but now, as the *Luftwaffe* became over-committed on each battle front in turn, the enemy fighter defences became much more difficult for the Stukas to penetrate.

The other means of countering the dive-bomber, which was now available in large and increasing quantities, was the fast-firing, medium-calibre anti-aircraft gun. Typical of the weapons in this class were the 40mm Bofors used by British forces and the 37mm M 1939 used by the Soviets. The weapons fired at a rate of about 120 rounds a minute, and a Ju 87 would be lucky to survive one hit from their explosive shells. Viewed from the target, a Stuka making a steep-diving attack appeared to hang almost stationary in space. It thus presented a zero-deflection shot, and if the gunners knew their business their fire was lethal.

By mid-1942 most high-value targets had effective gun defences, and the Stukas had to abandon their accurate steep-diving attacks. Increasingly they were used in shallow-dive or low-altitude attacks, which were less risky but also far less effective. Losses in experienced crews mounted rapidly, further reducing the effectiveness of those *Gruppen* equipped with the type. In the autumn of 1943 the *Sturzkampfgeschwader* (dive-bomber *Geschwader*) were renamed *Schlachtgeschwader* (ground attack *Geschwader*) and soon afterwards the majority of units re-equipped with FW 190 fighter-bombers. The day of the Stuka had passed.

CHAPTER THREE

Only One Came Back

When the Bristol Blenheim entered service with the Royal Air Force in 1937, the twin-engine bomber was one of the fastest combat aircraft in the world. Produced in large numbers, it formed a cornerstone of the Royal Air Force's rearmament programme. This was a time of rapid advances in aviation, however, and the Messerschmitt Bf 109E which entered service early in 1939 had a speed advantage of 70mph over the Blenheim. In the spring of 1940 the Blenheim squadrons were the mainstay of the RAF tactical bomber force, and they bore the brunt of the fighting when the Germans launched their offensive in the west. All of the units committed suffered heavy losses, none more so than No 82 Squadron when it attempted an attack on German troops advancing through Belgium on the morning of 17 May.

ON 10 MAY 1940, when the German offensive in the west opened, No 82 Squadron was based at Watton in Norfolk and had a strength of 22 Blenheim IV bombers. The unit spent the next two days on standby, awaiting the order to go into action. In the afternoon of 12 May it sent nine aircraft to bomb roads in Belgium, to crater them and render them impassable to enemy traffic. After another day of inactivity, in the morning of the 14th the Squadron sent six aircraft to attack rail and road targets in Holland. During these operations No 82 encountered no determined fighter opposition and all its aircraft returned safely.

Other units flying attack missions had suffered heavily, however, giving a grim foretaste of what lay in store if the slow bombers were intercepted by enemy fighters. In the afternoon of the 14th, the RAF tactical bomber squadrons launched an all-out attack on bridges over the Meuse River near Sedan, across which German troops and supplies were streaming to support the thrust into France. The area was patrolled by large numbers of Messerschmitts and the bombers suffered appalling losses: of the 71 aircraft taking part in the attacks, 40 were shot down. After the war the official historian would record that 'No higher rate of loss in an operation of comparable size has ever been experienced by the RAF'. Meanwhile No 82 Squadron's charmed existence continued. On the 15th it sent twelve aircraft to attack enemy troops concentrating near Montherme and again all of the Blenheims returned safely. The unit's run of luck was about to end, however, and do so in most brutal fashion.

At 2 a.m. in the morning of the 17 May, the crews were roused early and made their way to the briefing room. The unit had orders to bomb an enemy troop column reported to be moving between Namur and Gembloux in Belgium, the attack to be delivered at first light. It was still dark at 4.50 a.m. when Squadron Leader Miles Delap, the unit commander, led the first element of three bombers into the air off the grass runway at Watton. At measured intervals, the other three elements followed. Once airborne, Delap circled the airfield, lights on, while other elements formed up behind him. The formation comprised two flights each of six bombers with two elements flying in tight `vic' formation one behind the other and stepped down. Each aircraft carried four 250lb bombs. The Blenheims were to rendezvous en route with a squadron of Hurricanes that was to escort them to the target, but because of an administrative hitch the latter failed to show up. The Blenheims were to continue with their attack alone.

Cruising at 9,000ft on the clear spring morning, the raiders were nearing their target when suddenly they were buffeted by anti-aircraft shells bursting all around them. The formation opened out and the aircraft flew a weaving path to present a more difficult target for predicted fire. For one of the Blenheims the evasive action began too late, however, and the unfortunate machine fell out of the formation in a steep descent, trailing flames.

As suddenly as the cannonade began it ended, but this was the lull before the tempest. Before the bombers had time to regain their previous close formation, they came under attack from about fifteen Messerschmitt Bf 109s of *Jagdgeschwader 3* which dived from out of the sun and opened fire with cannon and machine guns. The Blenheims' gunners loosed off long bursts to try to beat off the fighters, but the bombers' light defensive armament was quite insufficient for the task. Delap later recalled:

Some of the bombers dived away, others went off weaving through the sky as they took evasive action. My own aircraft was holed along both the port and starboard wings and the port engine caught fire. Only the armour plating behind my seat saved me. Then a shell exploded in the cockpit and started a fire which produced so much smoke that I could no longer see the instrument panel. That was the last straw and I gave the order to bail out. With all that smoke I had no hope of reaching the floor escape hatch, so I released the hatch above my head and climbed up on my seat, facing aft, and prepared to jump clear. The next thing I knew, I was out in the cool air. After the heat and smoke in the cockpit that was quite a relief. Fortunately I was well covered and only my eyelashes had got burnt. When I was well clear of the aircraft I thought the time had come to pull the ripcord. I felt for it, but couldn't

---

BRISTOL BLENHEIM Mk IV

Role: Three-seat light bomber and reconnaissance aircraft.

Power: Two Bristol Mercury 9-cylinder, air-cooled, radial engines each developing 920hp at take-off.

Armament: Normal bomb load 1,000lb. (Defensive) one fixed Browning .303in machine gun firing forwards; two Browning .303in machine guns in the dorsal turret.

Performance: Maximum speed 266mph at 11,800ft; maximum cruising speed 225mph at 15,000ft.

Normal operational take-off weight: 14,500lb.

Dimensions: Span 56ft 4in; length 42ft 9in; wing area 469 sq ft.

Date of first production Blenheim IV: Spring 1939.

---

find it. I looked down for it, but it wasn't there. There was no panic, but I remember thinking 'That's odd!' Then I looked up and saw that parachute was already open. I hadn't lost consciousness and I knew I hadn't pulled the ripcord—it was indeed very odd.

The Messerschmitts had a field day, picking off the Blenheims one after another. That piloted by Sergeant 'Jock' Morrison was hit several times, one engine was knocked out and the aircraft and went into a spin. Probably the German fighter pilot thought it was going the same way as the others, and broke off the attack. Morrison regained control of the battered aircraft, however, levelled out close to the ground and set course for Watton flying on his remaining engine. It was the only bomber to survive the engagement.

After several minutes spent dangling from his parachute, Miles Delap was deposited gently in a forest:

> My parachute caught in a tree so I undid my harness and slid down the trunk. There was a battle going on nearby; I could not see anything but there was an exchange of small-arms fire not very far away. What was incongruous was that the birds were making nearly as much noise as the guns: it was about 6 o'clock in the morning and this was the dawn chorus. I had come down near Villiers, which seemed appropriate as it happens to be my middle name.

Soon after he had landed, the pilot was picked up by French soldiers, and eventually he returned to England via Cherbourg.

Delap knew that his force had suffered heavy losses, but not until he reached Watton a couple of weeks after the incident did he learn that only one Blenheim—Morrison's—had returned from the operation. And it had been damaged beyond repair. At Watton Delap was reunited with his navigator, Sergeant Frank Wyness, who had also returned from France. The latter was able to settle the mystery of Delap's missing ripcord. While the pilot had been standing on his seat, gathering his wits before jumping from the burning aircraft, Wyness thought he had lost consciousness. So he took hold of Delap's ripcord with one hand, and gave the pilot a hefty shove with the other. Then Wyness followed him out of the opening.

MESSERSCHMITT BF 109E-3

Role: Single-seat fighter.

Power: One Daimler Benz DB 601Aa 12-cylinder, liquid-cooled engine developing 1,175hp at take-off.

Armament: Two MF/FF 20mm cannon mounted in the wings; two MG 17 7.9mm machine guns mounted on top of the engine and synchronized to fire through the airscrew.

Performance: Maximum speed 348mph at 14,560ft; climb to 19,685ft, 6min 12sec.

Normal operational take-off weight: 5,875lb.

Dimensions: Span 32ft 4½in; length 28ft 4¼in; wing area 176.5 sq ft.

Date of first production E sub-type: February 1939.

Morrison and his crew, Delap, Wyness and the few others who made it back to Watton after parachuting into France had been the lucky ones. Of the 36 air crewmen who had set out on the attack, almost all had been killed or taken prisoner. None of their bombs had reached the intended target. It was a terrible example of the fate likely to befall those who fly obsolete aircraft against an enemy who possesses air superiority.

CHAPTER FOUR

Low Altitude Attack

Sunday 18 August 1940 saw some of the fiercest fighting of the Battle of Britain.
On that day the Luftwaffe planned heavy attacks on four important fighter air-
fields near London. The first of these, Kenley, was hit early that afternoon in an
action involving almost the whole of Kampfgeschwader 76.

DURING THE CAMPAIGNS in Poland and France, *Kampfgeschwader 76* had demonstrated its capabilities as a hard-hitting bomber unit. By the beginning of the Battle of Britain the *Geschwader* was established at three airfields situated near to each other to the north of Paris: *I* and *III Gruppen*, based at Beavais and Cormeilles-en-Vexin respectively, were equipped with Dornier Do 17s, and *II Gruppe*, based at Creil, had recently re-equipped with Junkers Ju 88s. Most crews in the *Geschwader* had previous combat experience, and morale was high.

The 9th *Staffel* of the *Geschwader*, part of *III Gruppe*, specialized in low-altitude attacks on pin-point targets. For the low-altitude attack role, the Do 17 was considered the best of the German twin-engine bomber types available. It was the only one powered by air-cooled radial engines, which were far less vulnerable to battle damage than their liquid-cooled equivalents. The aircraft of the 9th *Staffel* were fitted with additional armour to protect the crew and, to provide extra fire-power for engaging ground targets, each carried a 20mm Oerlikon cannon on a flexible mounting in the nose.

The attack on Kenley was planned to take place in three phases. First, a dozen Junkers Ju 88s of *II Gruppe* were to carry out a precision dive-bombing attack on the hangars and airfield installations. Five minutes later, 27 Dornier Do 17s of *I* and *III Gruppen* were to deliver a horizontal bombing attack from 12,000ft to crater the airfield and knock out the ground defences. The high-flying Ju 88s and Dorniers were to attack from the south-east and they would have full fighter es- cort. Finally, five minutes after the horizontal-bombing attack, nine Do 17s of the 9th *Staffel* were to run in at low altitude from the south to finish off any important buildings that were still standing. It was a bold and an imaginative plan but, like so many of its kind in the history of air warfare, it would be only partially suc- cessful. Only the low-altitude attack would cause serious damage, and in the pro- cess the 9th *Staffel* itself would suffer heavy losses. The account that follows will centre on the action fought by that unit.

Shortly before noon, the Dorniers and Ju 88s of the high-altitude raiding forces began taking off. The bombers assembled into formation and began their long, slow climb to attack altitude, heading for the Pas de Calais where they were to rendezvous with their escorting fighters. On the way the bombers ran into a layer

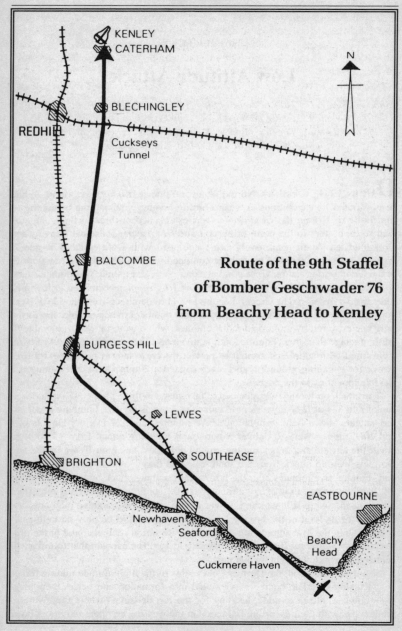

KENLEY
CATERHAM

BLECHINGLEY

REDHILL

Cuckseys
Tunnel

BALCOMBE

**Route of the 9th Staffel
of Bomber Geschwader 76
from Beachy Head to Kenley**

BURGESS HILL

LEWES

SOUTHEASE

BRIGHTON

EASTBOURNE

Newhaven

Seaford

Beachy
Head

Cuckmere Haven

N

of cloud that was much thicker than expected, with the result that several aircraft were forced out of formation. Above cloud the leaders had to orbit for several minutes to allow their formations to reassemble. At the time nobody realized it, but the delay was to have terrible consequences for the 9th *Staffel* attacking at low altitude.

Since it was to fly a more direct route to the target and remain at low altitude throughout the mission, the 9th *Staffel* left Cormeilles-en-Vexin several minutes after the other bombers. As usual during hazardous attacks, the unit's popular commander, *Hauptmann* Joachim Roth, flew as navigator in the leading Dornier. The nine-aircraft formation flew across northern France and the English Channel at a comfortable 500ft, letting down to 60ft to remain below the British radar cover as it approached the coast of Sussex.

Near the coast the bombers passed a couple of Royal Navy patrol boats, which opened an ineffective fire with machine guns. None of the Dorniers was hit and the boats were soon left behind. Soon after 1 p.m. the raiding force crossed the coast just west of Beachy Head.

In the light of what happened later, many Germans thought it was the chance meeting with the patrol boats that robbed the raiders of the advantage of surprise. The air defences of Great Britain rested on surer foundations than that, however. As the bombers neared the coast the Observer Corps post on top of Beachy Head reported their approach to the Observer Group Headquarters at Horsham: nine Dorniers at zero altitude, heading north-west. The report was relayed to Fighter Command's raid reporting net, and passed to each of the Group and Sector operations rooms.

Once past the coast, Roth continued on his north-westerly heading, making for Burgess Hill. He had chosen the small market town as his turning point because it lay on the junction of the rail lines from Lewes and Brighton, and from there he could follow the line to London; furthermore, the seven tall chimneys of the

---

DORNIER Do 17Z

Role: Four-seat bomber (with folding seat to enable one further person to be carried, if required).

Power: Two Bramo 323 Fafnir 9-cylinder, air-cooled, radial engines each developing 1,000hp at take-off.

Armament: Normal operational bomb load 2,200lb. (Defensive) six Rheinmetall Borsig MG 15 7.9mm machine guns in flexible mountings, two firing forwards, two firing rearwards and one firing from each side of the cabin. The aircraft operated by *9./KG 76* carried an Oerlikon 20mm cannon in place of one of the forward-firing machine guns.

Performance: Maximum speed 255mph at 13,120ft; normal formation cruising speed at 16,000ft, 180mph; normal formation cruising speed at low altitude (*9./KG 76*), 175mph; radius of action with normal bomb load, 205 miles.

Normal operational take-off weight: 18,930lb.

Dimensions: Span 59ft 0¼in; length 51ft 9½in; wing area 592 sq ft.

Date of first production Do 17Z: Early 1939.

PARACHUTE-AND-CABLE SYSTEM

Launched vertically into the path of low-flying aircraft, this unconventional weapon was fired in nine-round salvos from a row of launchers on the ground. The weapon comprised a 480ft length of steel cable suspended from a parachute, which opened automatically when the rocket reached the top of its climb at about 600ft. When an aircraft struck the cable and started to carry it forwards, the shock of the impact caused the opening of a second drag parachute attached to the bottom end of the cable. If the contraption snagged on the wing or any other part of the aircraft, the combined drag from the two parachutes imposed a violent deceleration that was usually sufficient to cause the machine to stall and fall out of the sky in an uncontrollable dive.

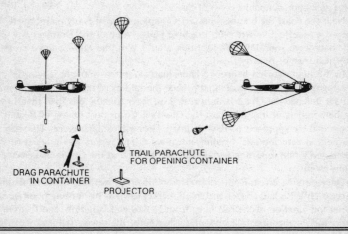

DRAG PARACHUTE
IN CONTAINER

TRAIL PARACHUTE
FOR OPENING CONTAINER

PROJECTOR

town's brickworks would serve as an unmistakable landmark for the low-flying aircraft. The bombers found Burgess Hill without difficulty and turned on to their northerly heading. As they roared low over the town, many of its citizens stood in the open, gazing up at the unaccustomed sight. *Unteroffizier* Günther Unger, piloting one of the Dorniers, recalled:

> At first they did not take us for the enemy, not expecting German aircraft to be flying so low. Then the large crosses on our wings taught them otherwise and in the next instant they were scurrying for cover.

Once past the town, the bombers raced northwards over the undulating countryside. War correspondent and photographer Rolf von Pebal, flying as a passenger in one of the Dorniers, later wrote:

> We zoomed over the English countryside, a few metres high. Every fold in the ground served as cover for us, each wood was exploited as a hiding place. We bounded over trees, undulating the whole time. A train rushed by underneath us. A couple of cyclists dashed for cover in the ditch by the side of the road.

The Observer Corps posts along the route continued to issue regular reports on the progress of the low-flying Dorniers. In the Sector operations room at Kenley, the station commander, Wing Commander Thomas Prickman, had watched as his two fighter squadrons were vectored to intercept the high-altitude raiding forces coming in from the south-east. When the 9th *Staffel* turned north over Burgess Hill, it was clear that his airfield or that at Croydon was under threat. Accordingly Prickman ordered all airworthy planes on the ground at Kenley to take off on a 'survival scramble' and head north-west, until the threat had passed. He also ordered No 111 Squadron, at readiness at Croydon with twelve Hurricanes, to scramble and patrol over Kenley at 3,000ft.

At 1.19 p.m. the Dorniers passed over the Reigate–Tonbridge railway line, one of the navigation features pointed out to crews at the briefing. Joachim Roth had achieved a clever piece of low-altitude navigation. After a 60-mile sea crossing and a flight of 40 minutes over unfamiliar enemy territory, he had brought his force to within three minutes of the target, on time and exactly on the planned route. But where were the pillars of smoke rising from the target, to indicate that the dive-bombing and horizontal attacks had subdued the airfield's defences? Obviously something had gone wrong, but Roth had every reason to believe that his unit still retained the advantage of surprise, and there was no thought of turning back.

At Kenley the anti-aircraft gun and rocket defences were stood-to and ready for action. The airfield's defence against low-flying aircraft comprised four 40mm Bofors guns, two obsolete 3in anti-aircraft guns and about twenty Lewis .303in machine guns. Also, along the northern edge of the airfield was a line of parachute-and-cable launchers, an unconventional 'secret weapon' that had not previously been used in action. Now, as the bombers closed in, the weapons were manned and loaded and the gun barrels were pointed expectantly to the south.

In the operations room at Kenley, Prickman watched the markers representing the enemy raiding forces march relentlessly across the map table towards his station. Now he ordered one of his officers to broadcast a final warning on the public address system: 'Air attack imminent: all personnel not on defence duties to the shelters.'

At 1.21 p.m., a couple of miles south of target, the Dorniers of the 9th *Staffel* leapt the final hundred feet to clear the North Downs and the formation widened out as the crews picked out their assigned targets. Moments later the Hurricane pilots of No 111 Squadron sighted the bombers and began curving into attack positions, while the German rear gunners let fly at them.

As this was happening, the Kenley ground defences opened fire with everything they had. There was the distinctive booming of the rapid-firing Bofors guns, as they loosed off bursts of six or eight rounds at a time. There was the louder, more measured bark of the 3in guns. Then came the stutter of one, then two, then several Lewis guns. In the Dorniers the gunners replied in kind, firing back with their cannon and machine guns.

The first aircraft to go down was a Hurricane, that flown by Flight Lieutenant Stanley Connors leading No 111 Squadron. Whether his fighter was hit by a bomber's return fire or by the Kenley defences, or by both, will never be known with certainty. The Hurricane swerved to one side and dived into the ground with the pilot still in the cockpit. The remaining Hurricanes pulled away violently to escape from the fiery inferno and headed round to the far side of the airfield to catch the bombers as they emerged from the target.

Günther Unger saw a hail of light flak and machine-gun fire shower past his cockpit. He pushed the aircraft yet lower and went for his target, the left-hand hangars. Moments later, Lewis-gun rounds thudded into his right engine and brought it to a smoking stop. The pilot feathered the propeller and struggled to hold the Dornier straight, as his navigator released the bombs in one long stick.

Unteroffizier Schumacher, piloting another of the Dorniers, watched the bombs from the leading aircraft ram into the hangars:

> Other bombs were bouncing down the runway like rubber balls. Hell was let loose. Then the bombs began their work of destruction. Three hangars collapsed like matchwood. Explosion followed explosion, flames leapt into the sky. It seemed as if my aircraft was grabbed by some giant.

Enemy rounds thudded into the bomber, leaving a smell of phosphorous and smouldering cables. Several of the plane's instruments were smashed, and the left engine was hit, belched smoke and started to lose power. As the Dornier leading the right-hand section was closing on its target, a Lewis-gun round hit the pilot squarely in the chest and he slumped forwards. The navigator, *Oberfeldwebel* Wilhelm Illg, leaned over the unconscious man and grabbed the control column to prevent the aircraft smashing into the ground.

After releasing their bombs on buildings on the south side of the airfield, the bombers skimmed low over the landing ground to make good their escape. Beside the line of parachute-and-cable launchers, the operator saw three enemy bombers coming straight for him and when he judged them to be within range he pushed his firing button. With a *whoosh*, a salvo of nine rockets soared into the sky, each leaving a trail of smoke. *Feldwebel* Wilhelm Raab was at the controls of one of the Dorniers heading towards the trails:

> Suddenly red-glowing balls rose up from the ground in front of me. Each one trailed a line of smoke about 1 metre thick behind it, with intervals of 10 to 15 metres between each. I had experienced machine-gun and flak fire often enough, but this was something entirely new.

Raab had no idea what was in front of him, but obviously the spectacle had not been laid on for his health. He eased the aircraft up from the ground, then swung the control wheel to the right to drop the right wing, to pass between two of the smoke trails:

> Everything seemed to be going well—then I felt a hefty tug on my machine. Now they've got us, I thought, we're going to smash into the ground.

HAWKER HURRICANE Mk I

Role: Single-seat fighter.
Power: One Rolls-Royce Merlin III 12-cylinder, liquid-cooled engine developing 1,030hp at 16,250ft.
Armament: Eight Browning .303in machine guns mounted in the wings.
Performance: Maximum speed 328mph at 20,000ft; climb to 20,000ft, 3min 30sec.
Normal operational take-off weight: 6,447lb.
Dimensions: Span 40ft; length 31ft 4in; wing area 258 sq ft.
Date of first production Hurricane I: October 1937.

But Raab's quick thinking had saved the Dornier from disaster. The aircraft was in a bank when it struck the cable, and the latter slid along the wing and fell clear before the lower parachute had time to open and take effect. Once through the line of smoke trails, Raab levelled out and waggled the controls; to his immense relief, the aircraft responded normally.

Another Dornier was less fortunate. It had been hit earlier and was on fire, and it ran straight into one of the hanging cables. The trap functioned as its designers intended and the combined drag of the two parachutes caused the bomber to stall and fall out of control. It smashed into the ground just beyond the airfield boundary and all five men on board were killed.

Joachim Roth in the leading Dornier was another of those threatened by the cables. He had released his bombs when the rockets rose into the sky in front of him. The pilot, *Oberleutnant* Rudolf Lamberty, eased the aircraft up a little to give more room to manoeuvre and turned to avoid the threat. In that he was successful, and the bomber cleared the obstacle easily. But immediately afterwards a Bofors shell struck the left wing beside the engine and blew a gaping hole in the structure. Petrol gushed from the shattered fuel tank and burst into flames, as Lamberty feathered the propeller of the dying engine and struggled to hold the Dornier in the air.

Lamberty passed over the airfield boundary, and immediately afterwards a pair of Hurricanes charged after him from above. The German pilot saw dust spurts rise from the ground in front of him, kicked up by bullets that had missed his aircraft. Those that hit the Dornier made a hollow sound 'like a handful of dried peas thrown against a window pane'. The first fighter overshot, then the other ran in to attack and scored further hits.

The Dornier was now a flying time-bomb: it was only a matter of time before the petrol fire burned through the main spar and the entire structure of the wing collapsed. The three crewmen in the rear cabin baled out, and two of them suffered broken limbs when they struck the ground with partially open parachutes. Lamberty crash-landed in a cornfield and he and Roth suffered burns during their escape from the plane.

With the formation broken up and most of the Dorniers under fighter attack, each bomber crew had to look to its own salvation. That said, however, the action that followed was not one-sided. The RAF pilots had no previous experience of engaging bombers manoeuvring close to the ground, while their opponents were at home in that environment. As a result, the Dornier crews were able to give as good as they got.

Sergeant Harry Newton swung his Hurricane into a firing position behind one of the bombers and saw tracer rounds coming towards him from his intended victim. The German pilot, Günther Unger, edged his Dornier lower to avoid the attack, but, flying on one engine, he had few options. Newton opened fire and saw his tracers go over the bomber's starboard wing:

> I thought, just a slight correction and I've got him! But just at that moment he got me, because my cockpit seemed to burst into flames . . . But I was so annoyed at the thought of that Dornier getting away that I put my hand back into the flames, groped for the stick, made my correction and then loosed off a long burst in the direction of where I thought the Dornier was.

Newton then pulled into an almost vertical climb to gain altitude before baling out, keeping his eyes tightly closed to protect them from the flames licking around him. The fighter's speed fell away rapidly, then the engine coughed to a halt. Newton slammed the stick forwards, kicked himself out of the cockpit and pulled his ripcord. As he did so he opened his eyes, in time to see the tail of his Hurricane flash past about a foot away from his right ear. The next thing he knew was that the parachute had opened and the ground was coming up to meet him.

The frenzied low-level chases over the Sussex countryside continued. In addition to the Hurricane shot down at the beginning of the action and that flown by Harry Newton, two other Hurricanes were hit and damaged by the bombers' return fire.

In an air action, events follow each other with great rapidity. Everything described in this narrative, from the time the 9th *Staffel* commenced its attack on Kenley until the last Hurricane broke off the chase, occurred in a space of just five minutes—from 1.22 to 1.27 p.m. on that fateful Sunday afternoon.

Seven of the nine Dorniers that had attacked Kenley re-crossed the south coast of England on their way home, but most were in a pitiful condition. Two of the bombers were each flying on a single damaged engine, and they ditched in the English Channel. Two more Dorniers with serious damage made it back to France but crash-landed near the coast; one was found to have no fewer than *two hundred hits* from .303in rounds, a testimony to the ruggedness of its structure. A further two Dorniers made wheels-down landings at airfields near the coast, one to allow a wounded crewman to receive medical attention, the other flown by its navigator after the pilot had been mortally wounded. Only one of the Dorniers returned without major damage or a seriously wounded crewman. Of the forty men on board the Dorniers, nine were killed, three were wounded and five were taken prisoner. All five officers taking part in the attack were killed, seriously wounded or captured. Never again would the *Luftwaffe* attempt a low-altitude, deep-penetration attack on a target in England with a formation of twin-engine bombers.

The low-altitude attack destroyed three out of the four hangars at Kenley, and several other buildings. The attack by horizontal bombers a few minutes later inflicted relatively little damage, except for some cratering of the landing ground. The two attacks destroyed four Hurricanes and a Blenheim fighter on the landing ground, and caused damage to two Hurricanes and a Spitfire. The planned attack on Kenley by Ju 88 dive-bombers failed to materialize. These aircraft arrived at the target late, to find the airfield shrouded in smoke from fires caused by the earlier attacks. They bombed their secondary target at West Malling airfield.

Although they inflicted severe damage, the attacks did not put Kenley airfield out of action for long. It was a relatively simple matter to select the least-cratered area of grass 500yds long and 50yds wide, render safe the unexploded bombs, fill in the craters and then flatten with a steam roller. Within a couple of hours, the airfield had a usable runway and limited fighter operations resumed; and within 24 hours of the attack, Kenley and her resident fighter squadrons were fully operational again.

* * *

There are three important operational lessons to be drawn from the attack on Kenley on 18 August 1940. The first is that low-flying aircraft are vulnerable to ground defences, if the former lose the element of surprise on their way to the target. That lesson is as true today as it was in 1940.

The second lesson is that resolute and well-equipped repair teams can restore an airfield to operations remarkably soon after an attack. Equipment that is destroyed or damaged can usually be replaced. Engineering work on aircraft can be carried out in the open, especially during the summer months.

The third lesson is that if there were a well-organized raid reporting system, it was extremely difficult to destroy fighters on the ground in any numbers by bombing their airfields. If there were sufficient warning—and during the Battle of Britain there usually was—fighters at a high state of readiness were airborne and clear of their base before an attack could develop. Aircraft dispersed on the ground or sitting in revetments were difficult to hit. The four RAF fighters destroyed on the ground during the attacks on Kenley represented a rare success for the German bomber force: during three and a half weeks of concentrated attacks on Fighter Command airfields in the Battle of Britain, *fewer than twenty* Spitfires and Hurricanes were destroyed on the ground at those airfields.

CHAPTER FIVE

Countering the Night Bomber

During August 1940 the Luftwaffe *began night attacks on cities in Great Britain, which ran in parallel with the daylight attacks on airfields during the Battle of Britain. So began the 'Night Blitz' that was cause enormous damage and large numbers of casualties. To counter this, the first-ever large-scale night bombing campaign, initially the British defences proved woefully inadequate and the raiders suffered minimal losses. Far more of the German planes were lost in flying accidents than were shot down by the defences. In the heat of battle the RAF had to try to cobble together an effective night air defence system, and by the end of the campaign it had succeeded.*

THE *LUFTWAFFE* BEGAN large-scale night raids on targets in Great Britain on 28 August 1940, when a force of 160 bombers was sent to attack Liverpool. The raiders returned to the port in similar strength on the three nights that followed, and also on the nights of 4, 5 and 6 September.

On 7 September the *Luftwaffe* shifted the focus of its attack to London, and that afternoon it sent a force of some 350 bombers escorted by more than 600 fighters to strike at the capital. The raid started huge fires in the dock areas to the east of the city, which were still burning that night when 318 bombers delivered a follow-up attack lasting lasted more than six hours. With their target clearly marked, the night raiders delivered their high-explosive and incendiary bombs with devastating accuracy. Soon after midnight there were nine fires raging that merited the official description of 'conflagration' (defined as a major fire that was spreading and which required more than 100 pumps to bring it under control). One such blaze, in the Surrey Docks, grew into the fiercest single fire ever recorded in Britain.

The fire brigades spent the whole of the daylight hours of the 8th in a desperate battle to control the fires, but several resisted their efforts to extinguish them. As a result, there was light aplenty to guide the 207 bombers which returned to the city after dark. The previous fires were fed afresh and new ones were kindled, and by dawn there were twelve conflagrations raging. A further 412 people had been were killed and 747 seriously injured. The bombers would be back in force on the following night and, with one exception due to bad weather, on every one of the sixty-five nights that followed.

Initially the night bombings could operate at will over Britain and their crews had little to fear from the defences. *Unteroffizier* Horst Goetz, a Heinkel 111 pilot with *Kampfgruppe 100*, recalled:

[45]

I have no particular memories of individual operations. They were all quite routine, like running a bus service. The London flak defences put on a great show—at night the exploding shells gave the place the appearance of bubbling pea soup. But very few of our aircraft were hit—I myself never picked up so much as a shell fragment. On rare occasions one of my crew might catch sight of a British night fighter, but it seems they never saw us and we were never attacked. During our return flights the radio operator would often tune in his receiver to a music programme, to provide some relief from the monotony.

The defending anti-aircraft gun and searchlight batteries relied mainly on sound locators to detect the bombers, but these gave only an imprecise indication of the whereabouts of an enemy plane, and if several aircraft were present in the area their engine noises swamped the locators. Few gun batteries had fire-control radar, and in any case this first-generation equipment had a low performance and its reliability was poor. On occasion the searchlights were effective as a means of pointing out targets for guns and night fighters, but they spent most of their time sweeping across the sky looking unsuccessfully for the bombers.

Under strong political pressure to 'do something' about the night raiders, General Frederick Pile, commanding the Army gun and searchlight units, ordered his gunners to maintain a steady fire when night raids were in progress, even if that meant firing off unaimed shells. If the gunners could not provide the substance of an effective defence, at least they would provide the sound of one. Ensconced in their shelters, the capital's citizens had no way of telling the difference. Later Pile would write on this type of engagement:

The volume of fire which resulted, and which was publicised as a 'barrage', was in fact largely wild and uncontrolled shooting. There were, however, two valuable results from it: the volume of fire had a deterrent effect upon at least some of the German aircrews . . . [and] there was also a marked improvement in civilian morale.

During September 1940 the gunners fired a quarter of a million anti-aircraft shells during the night engagements, most of them into thin air. They shot down less than a dozen enemy planes.

The defending fighter force was no better able to deal with the night raiders. A few twin-engine Blenheim fighters carried airborne interception (AI) radar, but the early equipment was crude and unreliable and the operators had to learn their craft from first principles. Moreover, the Blenheim had little margin of speed over the enemy planes it was supposed to catch. The other types then employed at night, the Spitfire, Hurricane and Defiant single-engine fighters, had the speed to catch the bombers but they lacked the radar necessary to find them.

The night fighter patrols spent many fruitless hours cruising around in the darkness, hoping for a chance sighting of an enemy aircraft. As yet there was no usable system for making controlled interceptions assisted by ground radar. The only help from the ground came from the searchlights which sometimes found their prey. Yet even when the bomber was illuminated in this way, it was still

difficult for a fighter crew to engage it. Pilot Officer Dick Haine, a Blenheim
night fighter pilot with No 600 Squadron, explained the problem:

> It might seem a simple matter for night fighter crews to see bombers which had
> been illuminated by searchlights, but this was not the case. If the raiders came on
> bright moonlight nights, which was usual during this time, the beams from the
> searchlights were not visible at heights much above 10,000 feet. If the searchlights
> were actually on the enemy bomber the latter could be seen from some way away,
> but only if the fighter was underneath the bomber and could see its illuminated
> underside; if the fighter was higher than the bomber, the latter remained invisible to
> the fighter pilot. If there was any haze or cloud it tended to diffuse the beams so
> that there was no clear intersection to be seen, even if two or more searchlights
> were accurately following the target.

For the future, Fighter Command had great hopes for the twin-engine Bristol
Beaufighter that had recently entered service. It was fast and had a good endurance, it carried a heavy armament of four 20mm cannon and six machine guns
and it was fitted with the latest Mk IV AI radar. However, the new fighter had
been rushed into production and it suffered from its fair share of teething troubles.
Some months would elapse before it was operational in sufficient numbers and
able to pose a serious threat to the night raiders.

In the meantime, the nightly attacks on London continued. Representative of
the heavier attacks on the capital was that on the night of 15/16 October. It was a
bright, moonlit night and the raiding force of some 400 bombers approached the
city at altitudes above 16,000ft. The vanguard of the raiding force came in from
the direction of Holland. Succeeding aircraft came in from Holland and Belgium
over the Thames Estuary, and from various points in northern France, crossing the
south coast of England between Bognor and Dungeness. The attack commenced
at 8.40 p.m. and German crews reported seeing heavy barrage fire over the capital, with shells detonating at altitudes between 13,000 and 20,000ft.

One of those taking part in the raid was Günther Unger, now a *Feldwebel*, in a
Do 17 of *Kampfgeschwader 76*. His crew was one of several that flew two sorties

---

BRISTOL BLENHEIM Mk IF

Role: Two-seat, long-range fighter and night fighter.

Power: Two Bristol Mercury XV 9-cylinder, air-cooled, radial engines each developing 840hp at take-off.

Armament: Five Browning .303in machine guns firing forwards; one Vickers K
.303in machine gun in the dorsal turret.

Performance: Maximum speed 260mph at 12,000ft; maximum cruising speed
220mph at 15,000ft; climb to 15,000ft, 15min.

Normal operational take-off weight: 13,800lb.

Dimensions: Span 56ft 4in; length 42ft 7in; wing area 469 sq ft.

Date of first production Blenheim I: February 1937.

Note: By the summer of 1940, some 30 of these aircraft were operational fitted with
AI Mk III radar.

---

that night, one on the evening of the 15th and one on the morning of the 16th. On both occasions their target was in the dock area of the city. Unger's orders were to circle over the target for as long as possible, releasing one bomb every few minutes to cause disruption on the ground over a long period. Untroubled by London's so-called gun 'barrage', Unger spent about twenty-five minutes circling over the target on each sortie.

Forty-one Royal Air Force fighters took off to engage the night raiders, but only two made interceptions. A Blenheim made radar contact with one of the bombers, but it lacked the speed to reach a firing position and after a lengthy chase the raider escaped. The other interception, by a Defiant of No 264 Squadron, was more successful. Pilot Officer Desmond Hughes was on patrol to the east of London when he caught sight of the enemy:

It was a bright moonlight night. Suddenly, out the corner of my eye I saw something move across the stars out to my left. If you are scanning the night sky it is normally completely still, so anything that moves attracts the eye. This just had to be another aircraft. I got Fred [Sgt Fred Gash, the gunner] to swing his turret round and we both kept an eye on the black shape. We moved towards it and soon caught sight of a row of exhausts. It was a twin-engined aircraft. I slid alongside, below and to the right of him, and slowly edged in 'under his armpit' while Fred kept his guns trained on the aircraft. Then we saw the distinctive wing and tail shape of a Heinkel—there was no mistaking it. I moved into a firing position, within about 50 yards of his wing tip and slightly below, so that Fred could align his guns for an upward shot at about 20 degrees. Obviously the German crew had not seen us—they continued straight ahead.

Fred fired straight into the starboard engine. One round in six was a tracer, but what told us we were hitting the Heinkel was the glitter of the de Wilde [incendiary] rounds as they ignited on impact. Fred fired, realigned, fired again. He got off two or three bursts. There was no return fire from the bomber—indeed, I doubt if any guns could have been brought to bear on our position on its beam. The engine burst into flames, then the Heinkel rolled on its back, went down steeply and crashed into a field near Brentwood.

BOULTON PAUL DEFIANT Mk I

Role: Two-seat turret fighter.

Power: One Rolls-Royce Merlin III 12-cylinder, liquid-cooled engine developing 990hp at 12,250ft.

Armament: Four Browning .303in machine guns mounted in a Boulton Paul hydraulically operated turret behind the cockpit.

Performance: Maximum speed 304mph at 17,000ft; climb to 15,750ft, 8min 30sec.

Normal operational take-off weight: 8,318lb.

Dimensions: Span 39ft 4in; length 35ft 4in; wing area 250 sq ft.

Date of first production Defiant I: July 1939.

Note: A few Defiants were fitted with AI radar, though these did not become operational until after the events described in this account.

The attack on the capital continued until 4.40 a.m. on the 16th and caused severe damage to the dock area and to the rail system. A bomb blew a large hole in the Fleet sewer, allowing the waters to escape and flood the rail tunnel between Farringdon Street and King's Cross stations. Becton gas works, Battersea Power Station and the BBC headquarters at Portland Place were hit, three large water mains were fractured and there was widespread damage in residential areas. More than 900 fires were reported in the capital, six of which were 'major' and nine 'serious'. London was not the only target that night: twenty Heinkels attacked Birmingham, while eight Dorniers raided .

The Heinkel that Hughes and Gash had shot down belonged to *Kampfgruppe 126* and was engaged in a minelaying operation over the Thames Estuary. Coincidentally, the only other German loss known to have been caused by the defences came from the same unit: it had been laying mines off the Suffolk coast when it struck a barrage balloon cable and crashed. The other German losses that night were probably the result of flying accidents. A Do 17 crashed on high ground in Wales, probably following a navigational error; another became lost, ran out of fuel and crashed near Wells. A Ju 88 crashed near Bishop's Stortford but its loss does not link with any claim made by the defences. In addition, six German bombers were wrecked in crashes or crash-landings in France and Holland.

* * *

As more Beaufighters were delivered to Fighter Command, and as the bugs were gradually ironed out of the aircraft and its equipment, the new fighter began to take an increasing toll of the night bombers. Also, early in 1941, the first ground-controlled interception (GCI) radars went into service. This radar was the first to employ the plan position indicator type of display, with the now-familiar rotating time-base. Using this equipment, a ground controller could see the juxtaposition of the night fighter and the bomber on his screen, and it was relatively

---

HEINKEL HE 111P-4

Role: Five-seat medium bomber.
Power: Two Daimler Benz DB 601A 12-cylinder, liquid-cooled engines each rated at 1,100hp at take-off.
Armament: Normal operational bomb load 3,300lb. (Defensive) Five Rheinmetall Borsig MG 15 7.9mm machine guns in flexible mountings, one firing forwards, one firing rearwards above the fuselage, one firing rearwards below the fuselage from the ventral position and two firing from the sides of the fuselage from waist positions; one 7.9mm in a fixed mounting, firing straight ahead.
Performance: Maximum speed 247mph at 16,400ft; normal cruising speed 190mph at 16,400ft; approximate radius of action (normal bomb load and operational fuel reserves) 350 miles.
Normal operational take-off weight: 29,760lb.
Dimensions: Span 74ft 1½in; length 53ft 9½in; wing area 943 sq ft.
Date of first production He 111P: Spring 1939.

easy to direct the former into a position to engage the latter. Gradually night fighting became a structured business, far removed from the hit-or-miss reliance on a chance meeting that Hughes and his gunners had exploited when they shot down their Heinkel.

To demonstrate the method of operation used by RAF night fighters from the spring of 1941, let us observe a typical interception of that period. At 2 a.m. on the morning of 9 July, *Oberleutnant* Hansgeorg Bätcher and his crew, flying a Heinkel He 111 of *Kampfgruppe 100*, were cruising over Somerset at 11,500ft, heading for their target at Birmingham. As the bomber neared the Bristol Channel it was tracked by the GCI radar station at Huntspill near Weston-super-Mare. Orbiting near the station, awaiting 'trade', was a Beaufighter of No 600 Squadron, crewed by Flying Officer R. Woodward and his radar operator Sergeant A. Lipscombe.

A series of vectors from the ground controller placed Woodward five miles behind the enemy plane and he was told to go to maximum speed to catch up. Shortly afterwards Lipscombe, peering at his radar screens, observed the return from the enemy aircraft just over two miles away. By then the Beaufighter had accelerated almost to its maximum speed and was overtaking the enemy plane too rapidly for a successful interception. Lipscombe told his pilot to throttle back, but again the speed correction was too great and as the Beaufighter slowed down the target disappeared off his radar screen. Woodward requested further help from the ground controller, and was again guided to within AI range.

By now both planes were north of Cardiff, heading north-east, with the Beaufighter again gaining slowly on the bomber. Woodward now takes up the story:

> After further vectors ending with 040°, [AI radar] contact was regained. Bandit [enemy aircraft] was then at 11,500 ft so I dived to 10,500 ft keeping the Bandit in contact dead ahead. Our speed then about 160 mph. A visual of a machine's exhausts was obtained about 1,000 ft above and ahead. Having identified the aircraft as Hostile I closed in climbing slowly to 300 feet and fired a three-second burst (with cannon and machine guns). No return fire was experienced. There was a blinding flash and explosion, and bits were seen to fly back. I gave another short burst before the enemy aircraft dived sharply to port with flames and smoke coming from its starboard side.

Hansgeorg Bätcher's recollection of the engagement links with the statements in Woodward's report. The first warning that the German crew had of the presence of the enemy fighter was when the ventral gunner suddenly shouted 'Night fighter . . . ' and the aircraft shuddered under the impact of exploding cannon shells. Bätcher jettisoned the bombs and hurled the aircraft into a diving turn, making for a cloud bank far below. Through the cupola over his position in the Beaufighter, Lipscombe watched the bomber diving away steeply with one engine on fire and disappear into cloud.

The speed of Bätcher's dive extinguished the flames before they took hold, and when he reached the cloud's enveloping folds he levelled out the bomber. As the German pilot took stock of the situation, however, it became clear that the Hein-

---

BRISTOL BEAUFIGHTER Mk I

Role: Two-seat, long-range fighter and night fighter.

Power: Two Bristol Hercules XI 14-cylinder, air-cooled, radial engines each developing 1,590hp at take-off.

Armament: Four Hispano 20mm cannon mounted in the nose; six Browning .303in machine guns mounted in the wings.

Performance: Maximum speed 323mph at 15,000ft; maximum cruising speed 272mph at 15,000ft; climb to 20,000ft, 14min 6sec.

Normal operational take-off weight: 20,800lb.

Dimensions: Span 57ft 10in; length 41ft 4in; wing area 503 sq ft.

Date of first production Beaufighter I: July 1940.

Note: During 1940 and 1941, night-fighter versions of the Beaufighter were fitted with Mk IV AI radar.

---

kel was in serious trouble. The ventral gunner was dead and the radio operator was badly wounded. The port engine was stopped and Bätcher feathered the windmilling propeller. The starboard engine had also suffered damage: it was running rough and developing only a fraction of its normal power. A large section of the rudder was shot away and, with the 'live' engine trying to push the Heinkel into a turn to the left, the pilot was unable to hold a straight heading; nor, on the available power, was it possible to maintain altitude. To add to the catalogue of woes, one of the fuel tanks had been punctured and was losing fuel and the main compass system no longer worked.

After some experimenting, Bätcher discovered a novel method of getting the crippled bomber to head in the general direction of France, albeit in a slow descent. Using the remains of the rudder, he held the aircraft on a southerly heading for as long as possible, then, when he could no longer hold it, he reversed the rudder and turned to the left through 300°. As it neared the required heading, he rolled out of the turn and held the required direction for as long as possible, then repeated the process. Using this 'two steps forward, one step back' technique and flying just above stalling speed, the Heinkel headed for France. The navigator tuned the radio compass to a beacon there to provide a heading reference.

Running the engine from the damaged tank, the latter was soon emptied. As more fuel was consumed the aircraft became progressively lighter, and the rate of sink gradually decreased. In the end Bätcher was able to maintain altitude, though by then the Heinkel was down to 1,200 feet. As yet more fuel was burned, the bomber became progressively easier to handle and the straight runs between the turns became progressively longer. In the end Bätcher was able to maintain the bomber on the desired heading. Shortly after reaching the coast near Cherbourg, the pilot put the battered Heinkel down on one of the landing grounds near the port.

On the basis of his observations, and the report from the ground controller at Huntspill who had seen the 'blip' from the enemy aircraft disappear off his radar screen in the dive, Woodward claimed the Heinkel as destroyed. No wreck could be found that linked with the claim, however, so the Beaufighter crew was credited only with an enemy bomber 'probably destroyed'. *Luftwaffe* records listed the Heinkel as 'damaged beyond repair', however, so Woodward's original claim was correct.

* * *

The essentials of radar-assisted night fighting were now in place. Meanwhile, the RAF night bomber force was building up its capability and the climax of the contest between it and the *Luftwaffe* night fighter force would occur in the spring of 1944. We shall observe this in some detail in Chapter 10, 'The Nuremberg Disaster'.

CHAPTER SIX

Battle of the Coral Sea

*The destructive attack by Japanese carrier-borne aircraft on the US Navy
fleet anchorage at Pearl Harbor in December 1941 established the aircraft
carrier as the dominant capital ship of the Pacific war. In the months that
followed, the nine Japanese and five American carriers were at sea for much
of the time, yet, such was the extent of the operational arena, a full half-year
elapsed before carrier battle groups faced each other in action. That
confrontation took place in May 1942, in the area of ocean between Australia and
New Guinea known as the Coral Sea. It would change the face of naval
warfare for all time.*

U P TO THE SPRING of 1942 there had been much conjecture, but little hard
evidence, about how carrier battle groups would fare if they met each other in action. Each of the larger US and Japanese carriers had a complement of more than
70 aircraft and could launch an extremely powerful air strike. There were many
who argued that an action of this type would resemble a huge suicide pact: both
sides would locate the other at about the same time and launch an air strike which
would sink or disable the other's carriers. When the surviving aircraft returned,
having no landing strip within range, they would come down in the sea and be
lost. Time and combat would reveal that, although this 'worst case' scenario
never actually happened, it was not far-fetched.

* * *

Of the aircraft types that equipped the front-line carrier squadrons at the beginning of the Pacific war, those of the Japanese Navy had the edge over those of the
US Navy. The difference was most marked in the case of torpedo bomber types.
The Japanese Nakajima B5N2 'Kate' was a fast, versatile and modern aircraft that
could serve with equal facility as a torpedo bomber, horizontal bomber or reconnaissance plane. The older American Douglas TBD Devastator was employed in
the torpedo- and horizontal-bombing roles, though because of its poor performance it was a good deal less effective than its enemy counterpart. The Japanese
superiority in aircraft was compounded by the greater effectiveness of the Type
91 air-launched torpedo compared with the American Bliss Leavitt Mk XIII. One
secret of the success of the Japanese weapon was the wooden air tail that stabil-
ized it in flight, allowing it to be released at speeds up to 185mph and from altitudes up to 500ft. The wooden tail broke away when the weapon struck the
surface, and in the water the torpedo had a running speed of 42kts. Lacking an air
tail, the Bliss Leavitt weapon had a maximum release speed of only 117mph and

---

NAKAJIMA B5N2 'KATE'

Role: Three-seat, carrier-based torpedo/horizontal bomber.
Power: One Nakajima Sakae 14-cylinder, air-cooled, radial engine developing 1,000hp at take-off.
Armament: (Offensive) One Type 97 torpedo or up to 1,650lb of bombs; (defensive) one Type 92 7.7mm machine gun on a hand-held mounting in the rear cabin.
Performance: Maximum speed 235mph at 9,850ft; cruising speed 164mph; normal attack speed and altitude for release of Type 97 torpedo, 185mph usually below 500ft.
Normal operational take-off weight: 8,360lb.
Dimensions: Span 50ft 11in; length 33ft 10in; wing area 412 sq ft.
Date of first production B5N2: Early 1941.

---

its maximum release altitude was 100ft. In the water the American torpedo had a running speed of only 33½kts, which meant that, unless the attack were pressed to short range, it was relatively easy for a fast-moving warship to avoid the torpedo.

As regards fighters, the Japanese Zero had a greater maximum speed and a better low-speed manoeuvrability than the American Wildcat, though the latter was the more manoeuvrable in high-speed combat and was a more rugged aircraft that could absorb greater punishment. The Japanese carrier fighter pilots began the Pacific war with the advantage of having had previous combat experience over China. By April 1942 this relative advantage had been eroded slightly, as US Navy pilots gained combat experience. The US Navy fighters had the advantage of a rudimentary system of interception control, using the early-warning radar sets fitted to their carriers. The Japanese carriers lacked radar and so had no warning of the approach of enemy aircraft until the latter came within visual range.

In terms of dive-bombers, the US Navy was the better off. The Douglas SBD Dauntless was a faster and generally more effective aircraft than the Japanese Aichi Type 99 'Val'. With the bombs removed, the Dauntless could even be used as a makeshift fighter to provide close-in defence for the carrier to ward off attacks by low-flying enemy torpedo bombers.

* * *

As April 1942 drew to a close, the Imperial Japanese forces had enjoyed a spell of unbroken victories lasting nearly five months. Large areas of south-east Asia and swathe of islands in the Pacific were now under their occupation, and forces were poised to launch new amphibious landing operations to expand the area under their control.

A large naval force under Vice-Admiral Shigeyoshi Inoue was about to set out to complete the occupation of New Guinea and seize the Solomon Islands and New Hebrides. A striking force formed around the large carriers *Shokaku* and *Zuikaku* (72 planes each), under the command of Rear-Admiral Chuichi Hara, was to provide distant cover for the operation and prevent the Allied navies from interfering. A separate naval force, including the small carrier *Shoho* (28 planes), was to provide close cover for the Japanese troop transports and their escorting ships.

While the Japanese Navy assembled its forces for the new thrust, US Navy cypher-breakers decoded parts of some signals relating to the operation. It was learned that three Japanese carriers were to take part, and Admiral Chester Nimitz, the US Pacific Fleet commander, saw this as an opportunity to strike a serious blow at the enemy. So long as the large Japanese carriers operated together as a unified force, they could overwhelm any carrier force the US Navy could assemble. Now three carriers had split away from the others to support the thrust into the South-West Pacific area (nothing in the decoded signals suggested that *Shoho* was smaller than the other two). Nimitz saw that if the enemy carriers could be surprised, there was a good chance of reducing the imbalance of naval power in the Pacific. Carefully, he and his staff laid plans for a counter-strike. The US Navy carrier *Yorktown* (72 planes), with three cruisers and six destroyers, was already in the south Pacific area; *Lexington* (71 planes), with two cruisers and five destroyers, was ordered to run from Pearl Harbor to join her. On 1 May the two carriers and their escorts linked up in the eastern part of the Coral Sea, and Rear-Admiral Frank Fletcher in *Yorktown* assumed overall command of the force.

During the night of the 5th/6th, the Japanese strike carrier force passed round the eastern end of the Solomon Islands and into the Coral Sea, moving into position to block any attempt to interfere with the amphibious landings. Throughout 6 May a deep depression lay over the stretch of ocean, giving continuous and dense cloud cover and frequent rain showers. Reconnaissance planes from both sides scoured the area for the opposing warships but, since none of the planes carried radar, almost all were unsuccessful. The sole exception was a Japanese land-based aircraft from Rabaul which found part of Fletcher's force during the morning; but then, because of delays in re-transmitting the report to Hara's flagship, the report would not reach the Japanese commander until the following day.

Both sides realized that the enemy had a strong naval force in the area, though both were ignorant of their opponent's whereabouts and, in the Japanese case,

---

DOUGLAS TBD DEVASTATOR

Role: Three-seat, carrier-based torpedo/horizontal bomber.

Power: One Pratt & Whitney R-1830-64 Twin Wasp 14-cylinder, air-cooled, radial engine developing 900hp at take-off.

Armament: (Offensive) One Mk XIII Bliss Leavitt torpedo or two 500lb bombs; one Browning .5in or .3in machine gun mounted on the starboard side of the fuselage and synchronized to fire through the airscrew. (Defensive) One Browning .3in machine gun on a hand-held mounting in the rear cabin.

Performance: Maximum speed 206mph at 8,000ft; cruising speed 128mph; maximum attack speed and altitude for release of Mk XIII torpedo, 117mph and 100ft.

Normal operational take-off weight: 9,289lb.

Dimensions: Span 50ft; length 35ft; wing area 422 sq ft.

Date of first production TBD: June 1937.

MITSUBISHI A6M2 MODEL 21 (ZERO)

Role: Single-seat, carrier-based fighter.

Power: One Nakajima Sakae 12 14-cylinder, air-cooled, radial engine developing 950hp at take-off.

Armament: Two Type 99 Model 1 Mk 4 20mm cannon (German Oerlikon built under licence) mounted in the wings; two Type 89 7.7mm machine guns (near-copies of the WWI British Vickers) mounted above the engine and synchronized to fire through the airscrew; provision to carry two 132lb bombs on underwing racks.

Performance: Maximum speed 331mph at 14,930ft; climb to 19,672ft, 7min 27sec.

Normal operational take-off weight: 5,134lb.

Dimensions: Span 39ft 4½in; length 29ft 8½in; wing area 241.5 sq ft.

Date of first production A6M2: February 1941.

Note: Lacking information on the designations of the Japanese aircraft they were meeting in combat, the Western Allies allocated boys' names to fighters and girls' to bombers. Under this system, the Zero was renamed the 'Zeke'; but the old name stuck, and many people continued to refer to the aircraft as the Zero.

---

their exact composition. The opposing carrier forces behaved like a couple of short-sighted prize fighters, moving warily around the ring and squinting for some sign of the other, ready to throw a punch. (After the war, the two sides' charts of the action were compared, and it was seen that at one point that day the opposing carrier groups passed within 70 miles of each other without either detecting the other's presence.)

At dawn on 7 May tension in the area was high. By then the Japanese commander knew he was opposed by forces that included at least one enemy carrier and perhaps two. Both sides saw that a clash was imminent and both launched several reconnaissance planes to comb the area for the enemy. Low cloud still made life difficult for the searchers, however, and led to inaccurate reporting. Early that morning a Japanese scouting plane reported that it had sighted an enemy aircraft carrier in company with a cruiser, at a position 160 miles south of the Japanese striking force. (Because of the poor visibility, the report was quite inaccurate: the ships were in fact the US fleet oiler *Neosho* and the destroyer *Sims*.)

Without waiting for a confirming report from a second plane sent into the area, the Japanese admiral turned to close the distance and launched a striking force comprising 25 B5N ('Kate') horizontal bombers and 36 D3A ('Val') dive-bombers, with an escort of eighteen Zero fighters. Soon after these set out, another Japanese reconnaissance aircraft reported (correctly) the sighting of a enemy carrier and ten other vessels about 280 miles to the *north-west* of the main Japanese carrier force.

The second report raised doubts in Hara's mind, but the distance of the enemy from his force ruled out an immediate air strike from or against his carriers. He decided to let his planes continue with their briefed attack, and when they returned he would prepare a new striking force as soon as possible. Meanwhile Admiral Fletcher, the US carrier commander, had also been misled by an inaccurate reconnaissance report from one of his aircraft. He received a report of two enemy carriers and four heavy cruisers at a position some 225 miles to the *north-west* of his force. (The message should have read 'two heavy cruisers and two destroyers', but there had been an encoding error before transmission; and even the 'correct' message was in error, for in fact the enemy force comprised only two light cruisers and two armed merchant ships.)

Accepting the report at its face value and assuming that it referred to the main Japanese carrier group, Fletcher launched a striking force of 52 dive-bombers and 22 torpedo bombers with an escort of eighteen fighters to attack the enemy 'carriers'. They were airborne when the reconnaissance crew landed on *Yorktown*, and only when they made their verbal report of the mission did the error become clear. To his great chagrin, the US commander learned that he had committed his striking force against what seemed to be a target of relatively minor importance. But, like Hara, Fletcher decided that he had little to gain by ordering the planes to abandon the attack and return.

When the Japanese air striking force reached the area where the enemy 'carrier' and 'cruiser' had been reported, they found only the oiler and the destroyer. With no more lucrative target available, the aircraft vented their spleen on the two ships, sinking *Sims* and leaving *Neosho* ablaze.

As the Japanese planes and their disappointed crews headed back to their carriers, the American air striking force was much more fortunate. By chance, Dauntless bombers scouting ahead of the main attack force chanced upon the Japanese carrier *Shoho*, in an area of clear skies and coincidentally only 35 miles from the position of the erroneously reported carrier. The main striking force was summoned to the scene and the small carrier was overwhelmed by the attack. *Shoho* was soon reduced to a wreck, listing to starboard and burning furiously, but aircraft continued to pound the vessel. Devastators closed to short range to launch torpedoes at the slow-moving target, and under these optimum conditions even the Mk XIII was able to wreak great damage. It is estimated that the light carrier took hits from thirteen bombs and seven torpedoes before she capsized and sank.

Meanwhile, some 300 miles south of the *Shoho* action, the Japanese planes were returning to the two larger carriers after attacking *Sims* and *Neosho*. As soon

---

GRUMMAN F4F-4 WILDCAT

Role: Single-seat, carrier-based fighter.

Power: One Pratt & Whitney R-1830-86 Twin Wasp 14-cylinder, air-cooled, radial engine developing 1,200hp at take-off.

Armament: Six Browning .5in machine guns mounted in the wings.

Performance: Maximum speed 320mph at 18,800ft; climb to 20,000ft, 12min 24sec.

Normal operational take-off weight: 7,975lb.

Dimensions: Span 38ft; length 29ft; wing area 260 sq ft.

Date of first production F4F: Late 1940.

as all had landed, the deck crews repositioned the aircraft aft and began working furiously to refuel and re-arm those planes earmarked for a next air strike. Rear-Admiral Hara received a radio report of the loss of *Shoho* and, from the number of American aircraft involved, it was clear that his enemy had at least two carriers were in the area.

It was late in the afternoon before the Japanese aircraft were ready for launch for their second strike, which meant that the earliest that they could attack the enemy carriers would be at dusk, and that the planes would return after dark. Flown by crews chosen for their skill and experience, twelve D3A dive-bombers and fifteen B5N torpedo bombers took off from *Zuikaku* and *Shokaku* at 4.30 p.m. and headed for the position where the American carriers had been reported. The weather in the area remained poor, however, and the Japanese planes flew past their intended targets without sighting them. The aircraft continued on, almost to the limit of their endurance, and carried out a brief search; then, having found nothing, they jettisoned their ordnance and turned back for their carriers.

During the return flight, some of the Japanese planes came within range of the CXAM early-warning radars fitted to *Yorktown* and *Lexington*, and Wildcat fighters were vectored into position to intercept them. In the ensuing combats, nine Japanese and two American planes were shot down.

Darkness came quickly in those latitudes, and the Japanese crews, many of them near to exhaustion having flown two exacting missions since dawn, had great difficulty in regaining their carriers. Aircraft returned individually, and in the gloom five crews mistook *Yorktown* for one of their own carriers and circled the ship in preparation to landing. Only when the carrier and her escorts put up a withering defensive fire, which forced them to break away violently, did the men realize their error. Those Japanese aircraft that regained their carriers arrived with their tanks almost empty, and several planes ran out of fuel and splashed into the sea. Of the 27 aircraft that set out to attack the American carriers, only six landed safely.

So ended 7 May, the first occasion on which aircraft carriers had fought against their own kind. Clearly, the day had gone to the US Navy. *Shoho* had been sunk with all of her planes and, adding these planes to those lost during the abortive dusk raid, the Japanese force was now weaker by 49 aircraft. For their part, the American carriers had lost only six aircraft. The higher Japanese losses left the opposing carrier-borne units almost exactly equal in numerical strength: both now had about 130 aircraft operating from two large carriers.

During the small hours of 8 May both sides again prepared to fight a major fleet action, and all four carriers had striking forces drawn up on their after deck with planes fuelled, armed and ready to launch. Shortly before dawn the carriers dispatched reconnaissance planes to re-scour the ocean for the enemy. Now nothing mattered except for the enemy carriers, and other surface vessels were of importance only in so far as they could influence the carrier-versus-carrier action about to unfold.

Rear-Admiral Hara decided not to wait for the sighting report to come in, and at 8 a.m. he launched 33 dive-bombers, eighteen torpedo bombers and eighteen

AICHI TYPE 99 'VAL'

Role: Two-seat, carrier-based dive-bomber.
Power: One Mitsubishi Kinsei 44 14-cylinder, air-cooled, radial engine developing 1,070hp at take-off.
Armament: (Offensive) One 550lb bomb under the fuselage; provision for up to four 66lb bombs on underwing racks; two Type 97 7.7mm machine guns mounted above the engine and synchronized to fire through the airscrew. (Defensive) One Type 7.7mm machine gun on a flexible mounting at the rear of the cabin.
Performance: Maximum speed 237mph at 9,845ft; cruising speed 184mph.
Normal operational take-off weight: 8,378lb.
Dimensions: Span 47ft 1¼in; length 33ft 1¾in; wing area 376.5 sq ft.
Date of first production Type 99: Late 1940.

Zeros and sent them to the area where he expected the enemy to be. In the event, reconnaissance aircraft from both sides located the opposing carriers at about the same time, and their sighting reports reached their respective commanders shortly after 8.30 a.m. The opposing forces were then about 210 miles apart, the Japanese carriers being to the north-north-west of the American ships. Fletcher launched two striking forces comprising 48 Dauntlesses and 21 Devastators with an escort of sixteen Wildcats. The Japanese striking force, already airborne, turned to make for the area where the American carriers had been found.

The opposing striking forces passed in mid-air without either seeing the other. The first to go into action were planes from the *Yorktown*, whose dive-bombers sighted the main Japanese carrier force through a break in the cloud. While the dive-bombers circled, waiting for the slower torpedo bombers to move into position to attack at low altitude, *Zuikaku* headed into a rain squall and nothing more was seen of her. *Shokaku*, about six miles to the east and in an area of clear skies, turned into the wind preparatory to launching her fighters.

As the American torpedo bombers began their attack runs on *Shokaku*, and with the escorting Wildcats doing their best to hold off the Zeros, *Yorktown*'s 24 Dauntlesses rolled into their attack-dives at 17,000ft and continued down to 2,500ft. Each plane released a single 1,000lb bomb. Although the American crews

DOUGLAS SBD-2 DAUNTLESS

Role: Two-seat, carrier-based dive-bomber and scout aircraft.
Power: One Wright R-1820-52 Cyclone 14-cylinder, air-cooled, radial engine developing 1,000hp at take-off.
Armament: (Offensive) Normal load for attacks on warships, one 1,000lb armour-piercing bomb; two Browning .5in machine guns mounted above the engine and synchronized to fire through the airscrew. (Defensive) Two Browning .3in machine guns on a hand-held mounting in the rear cabin.
Performance: Maximum speed 250mph at 8,000ft; cruising speed 152mph.
Normal operational take-off weight: 10,400lb.
Dimensions: Span 41ft 6in; length 32ft 8in; wing area 325 sq ft.
Date of first production SBD: June 1940.

IMPERIAL JAPANESE NAVY SHIP *SHOKAKU*

Role: Aircraft carrier.
Displacement: 29,800 tons.
Maximum speed: 34 kts.
Defensive armament: Sixteen 5in guns; forty-two 25mm anti-aircraft guns.
Crew: 1,660.
Flight deck: Length 844ft; beam 85ft 4in.
Complement of aircraft at start of Coral Sea action: 18 Mitsubishi A6M2 Zero fighters; 27 Aichi D3A ('Val') dive-bombers; 27 Nakajima B5N ('Kate') torpedo/horizontal bombers.
Date of commissioning: Late 1941.

USS *LEXINGTON*

Role: Aircraft carrier.
Displacement: 33,000 tons.
Maximum speed: 34kts.
Defensive armament: Eight 5in guns; 105 20mm and 40mm anti-aircraft guns.
Crew: 3,300.
Flight deck: Length 888ft; beam 105ft.
Complement of aircraft at start of Coral Sea action: 23 F4F-3 Wildcat fighters; 36 SBD Dauntless dive-bombers; 12 TBD Devastator torpedo bombers.
Date of commissioning: 1927.

---

claimed six certain and three probable hits on the carrier, from Japanese records it is clear that the vessel received only two direct hits. Making good use of cloud cover, the dive-bombers withdrew without loss. Then the nine Devastators from *Yorktown* closed in to launch their torpedoes, under heavy fire from the Japanese carrier and her escorting cruisers. The attack was carried through bravely, but, although the crews claimed three or possibly four hits on the carrier, in fact these weapons caused no damage. The Mk XIII lived down to its reputation that day, and it is clear that the torpedoes either missed the target or, if they hit it, failed to explode (the torpedo had a notoriously unreliable firing system). Arriving ten minutes later, *Lexington*'s air group was less successful and the main force of dive-bombers failed to find a target. Only four Dauntlesses and eleven Devastators found *Shokaku* and attacked her, and they achieved only a single bomb hit.

Although their ship had suffered serious damage from the three bomb hits, the damage control teams on the Japanese carrier soon brought under control the fires started by the explosions. *Shokaku* was unable to continue operational flying and she left the area under her own steam for the naval base at Truk.

The scene shifts to the two American carriers, which were bracing themselves for a powerful attack from Japanese planes. This time luck was on the side of the latter, whose crews arrived to find clear skies and the large ships visible from 50 miles or more. *Lexington*'s radar operators detected the incoming aircraft from about 75 miles, but the rudimentary equipment provided no indication of height and the fighter controllers failed to position the few available Wildcats effectively. Eight American fighters patrolled at 10,000ft and nine more fighters were launched to join them. To stiffen the defence, a dozen Dauntlesses orbited each carrier three miles away at about 2,000ft. These planes were to pounce on enemy torpedo bombers heading for the carriers (although it was clearly no match for a Zero, a Dauntless without bombs was a formidable opponent for a heavily laden torpedo bomber committed to a long, straight attack run).

As the 'Vals' and 'Kates' delivered their attacks, the American carriers manoeuvred independently to avoid the enemy torpedoes and bombs. *Yorktown* successfully avoided all eight of the torpedoes aimed at her, and all but one of the bombs. The latter struck near the island and penetrated four decks before exploding, causing considerable damage; the ship's flight deck was undamaged, however, and aircraft continued taking off and landing. *Lexington*, larger and less manoeuvrable than *Yorktown*, was less fortunate. She took two torpedo hits on the port side and suffered two bomb hits. Nevertheless, the doughty warship continued to fight back. Within minutes of the end of the attack, her damage control teams had halted the flooding, and her 7-degree list was corrected by moving fuel oil to tanks on the starboard side. Then, about an hour after the attack, as the carrier was recovering aircraft, disaster struck. A huge internal explosion ripped through her vitals, caused by the ignition of petrol fumes leaking from a ruptured aviation fuel tank. The explosion was followed by a series of smaller ones, and within a short time there were fires blazing in several parts of the ship. Those of her aircraft that were still airborne were ordered to land on *Yorktown*. *Lexington*'s crew fought a losing battle to bring the fires under control, but in the end her captain ordered the escorting destroyers to come alongside and take off the crew. Later that evening one of the destroyers finished off the abandoned carrier with a salvo of torpedoes.

By now both sides were down to one usable carrier. Neither commander felt that he was in a position to continue the fight, and both headed away from the area. *Zuikaku* had emerged from the action unscathed, but her air group was reduced to 39 planes. *Yorktown*, having taken on several of *Lexington*'s planes, now had 64 aircraft, but, owing to internal damage from the bomb hit, her operational ability was limited.

* * *

So ended the Battle of the Coral Sea. In the short term, it was a victory for the Japanese Navy, for the loss of *Lexington* and the damage to *Yorktown* far outweighed the loss of the smaller *Shoho* and the damage to *Shokaku*. In terms of aircraft losses, including those that went down when their carrier was sunk, the figures were nearly equal—77 US carrier planes compared with 87 Japanese Navy machines.

In action, the big carriers were found to be relatively easy to damage but extremely difficult to sink. The main lesson of the loss of *Lexington*—the need for improved damage control techniques and a more effective venting system for potentially explosive fumes—would be well learned, and her successors would profit from it. Taking the effect of the battle on the Pacific war as a whole, the Americans were the long-term victors. They had thwarted a full-blooded Japanese invasion attempt and delayed the enemy advance into the south Pacific for several months. The lengthy repairs necessary for *Shokaku*, and the need to reform *Zuikaku*'s depleted air group, kept both of these important carriers out of action during the decisive battle near Midway two months later. *Yorktown*'s damage was rapidly repaired at Pearl Harbor, and she played an important role in the Battle of Midway before she met her end there. In terms of morale, the Battle of the Coral Sea marked a watershed for those trying to stem the Japanese advance through the Pacific: it was the first major action in which Japanese forces had not been victorious and had, moreover, suffered serious losses.

As has been said, the Battle of the Coral Sea was the first naval engagement to be fought solely between carrier-based aircraft. It established the pattern for naval actions in that theatre—a pattern that would continue until the Japanese Navy had no operational aircraft carriers left.

CHAPTER SEVEN

Battle of the Bay

'The Bay' was the Bay of Biscay, the area of sea between Brest on the north-west coast of France and Cape Ortegal on the north-west coast of Spain. 'The Battle' took place in the strip of water running from the western edge of the Bay into the Atlantic. For much of the Second World War this waterway was of great strategic importance, for U-boats sent to attack the Allied transatlantic convoys had to pass through it twice on each sortie as they ran out from and returned to their bases. The contestants in the campaign were the German U-boats on the one side and the maritime patrol aircraft of RAF Coastal Command on the other. The hardest-fought phase took place between June 1942 and October 1943 and saw actions unique in the history of air warfare. Air crews flew large numbers of hours but only rarely did they engage their enemy. When engagements did take place, they were often characterized by great ferocity and considerable personal bravery. Moreover, to a degree rarely equalled in other types of air action, there were continual technological and tactical thrusts and counter-thrusts as each side sought to gain an advantage, often temporary, over its adversary.

EARLY IN 1941, as RAF Coastal Command built up in strength and its aircraft were fitted with radar and improved anti-submarine weapons, the air patrols over the Bay of Biscay became progressively more of a threat for the U-boats traversing the waterway. The German crews found that the easiest way to avoid the air patrols was to remain submerged during the day and run on the surface at night, using the diesel engines to recharge the boat's batteries.

At night, the submariners knew, they were safe from air attack on the surface. Although many of the aircraft carried air-to-surface vessel (ASV) Mk II radar, which could detect submarines on the surface, a night attack had little prospect of success. The depth charges had to be released from low level, and when a low-flying aircraft came within about a mile of a U-boat, the latter's echo signals merged into the 'sea clutter' on the radar screen and nothing more was seen of it.

If its aircraft were to deliver successful night attacks on U-boats, Coastal Command desperately needed some means of maintaining contact with the target during the all-important final mile of the attack run. The solution to the problem was a modified naval 24in searchlight that could be lowered under the fuselage of the Wellington bomber, using the installation originally built for the aircraft's retractable ventral gun position. The searchlight put out a narrow but intense beam, which could be trained on to the U-boat and held on it by an operator in the nose of the aircraft using a hydraulic control system. The device was called the 'Leigh Light', after its inventor Squadron Leader Humphrey Leigh. In the spring of 1941 a Leigh Light Wellington carried out a series of mock attacks at night on a Royal Navy submarine, and these demonstrated that the searchlight was of considerable assistance, though it required some modification before it was suitable for operational use. It took some months to perfect the system and put it into production.

Early in 1942 No 172 Squadron was formed to carry out night attacks on U-boats, and the unit received its first Wellington VIII aircraft fitted with a Leigh Light. The crews began a period of intensive training in the difficult and potentially dangerous business of delivering low-level attacks at night. By the beginning of June the Squadron possessed five Leigh Light Wellingtons and several crews proficient in the precise flying necessary to attack targets illuminated by the searchlight.

The Leigh Light was first used in action during the early morning darkness of 4 June, when Squadron Leader Jeff Greswell and his crew attacked the Italian submarine *Luigi Torelli* on the surface as she was heading into the Atlantic. The boat suffered severe damage which forced her to abandon her patrol.

In the course of June, the Squadron attacked five enemy submarines on the surface at night. The first Leigh Light attack to result in the loss of a U-boat was during the night of 5/6 July, when Pilot Officer W. Howell and his crew caught *U502* on her way home after a successful foray in the Caribbean. Just over a week later this crew carried out another successful Leigh Light attack and inflicted serious damage on *U159*.

In the initial two months of operations with the Leigh Light, the five modified Wellingtons had an effect on the enemy that went far beyond their achievement of one submarine sunk and two damaged. The U-boat crews had lost the immunity they had previously enjoyed while crossing the Bay at night on the surface: now they were liable to suffer sudden and demoralizing attack from the air without warning. The U-boat crews coined their own epithet for the Leigh Light: '*Das verdammte Licht!*' ('That damned light!').

In July *Admiral* Karl Dönitz, the commander of the U-boat force, reacted to the new situation by ordering his crews to reverse their previous procedure for cros-

---

VICKERS WELLINGTON Mk VIII

Role: Six-seat maritime patrol aircraft.

Power: Two Bristol Pegasus XVIII 14-cylinder, air-cooled, radial engines each developing 1,050hp at take-off.

Armament: Normal operational load eight 250lb depth charges; one hand-held Vickers K .303in machine gun in the nose; two Browning .303in machine guns in the powered rear turret.

Performance: Maximum speed 235mph at 15,500ft; attack speed 172mph at 50ft; normal patrol speed 130mph at 2,000ft; typical radius of action (normal weapon load) 700 miles.

Normal operational take-off weight: 30,000lb.

Dimensions: Span 86ft 2in; length 64ft 7in; wing area 640 sq ft.

Date of first production Wellington VIII: Late 1941.

Note: Aircraft fitted with ASV Mk II radar and Leigh Light in the rear fuselage.

U966 (TYPE VIIC U-BOAT)

Surface displacement: 769 tons.

Armament: (Offensive) Four bow and one stern torpedo tubes with fourteen 533mm torpedoes (770lb warheads); (defensive, mid-1943) four 20mm cannon in two paired installations and one 37mm cannon, mounted on platforms to the rear of the conning tower.

Performance: Maximum speed (surface, diesel engines) 17kts, (submerged, electric motors) 7kts; endurance (surface) 6,500nm at 12kts, (submerged) 80nm at 4kts; minimum time to submerge 50sec; maximum safe diving depth 650ft.

Dimensions: Length 220ft 3in; beam 20ft 4in.

Date of first Type VIIC U-boat: Early 1941.

---

sing the Bay: from now on they were to traverse the stretch of water submerged at night and run *on the surface by day*. By day, the argument ran, the boats' lookouts would have a better chance of seeing the aircraft and initiating a crash-dive before an attack developed. The change of tactics gave the Coastal Command daylight air patrols a rare chance to find their enemy, and they seized it eagerly. In August there were 34 sightings of U-boats running on the surface by day in the Bay area, and in September there were 37. Between the beginning of June and the end of September the daylight air patrols sank four U-boats and caused damage to several others, in many cases forcing them to abandon their patrols and return to base.

German naval intelligence officers had long known that the attacking aircraft relied on ASV radar to detect U-boats on the surface, and this device was seen as an essential element of the night attacks. The answer was to fit U-boats with a simple receiver that could pick up the ASV emissions and warn crews of the proximity of enemy aircraft. The boats could then dive out of harm's way, and resume their run on the surface when the danger had passed. Named after the company that built it, the *Metox* warning receiver was introduced in September 1942, and by the end of the year nearly every operational U-boat carried one. The device restored to the submariners the invulnerability that they had enjoyed when running on the surface at night: in September the air patrols made only two sightings of U-boats on the surface in the Bay, and in the following month there were none.

By the end of 1942, however, the patrol planes were about to introduce to service two new and advanced types of airborne radar, the British ASV Mk III and the American SCR-517. The new radars could locate submarines on the surface at longer ranges and with greater precision than the earlier equipment. Moreover—and significantly in the light of the German countermeasures—the band of microwave frequencies in which the new radars operated lay outside the range of cover of the *Metox*.

Early in 1943 No 172 Squadron re-equipped with the newer Mk XII Wellington fitted with ASV Mk III radar. For U-boat crews there was a resumption of the unannounced night attacks which had devastated morale the previous year. In

March and April 1943 the aircraft sank only two U-boats at night, but the crews of several others returned with hair-raising tales of the narrow escapes.

Pending the introduction of a new warning receiver that would pick up the signals from microwave radars, at the end of April *Admiral* Dönitz again issued orders that boats crossing the Bay of Biscay should remain submerged at night and run on the surface by day. Also, during their refits between sorties, the boats were fitted with batteries of 20mm cannon, and in some cases 37mm weapons, so that those caught on the surface could drive off their tormentors.

Again, the change in German tactics was immediately obvious to those flying the daylight patrols over the Bay. In the first week in May 1943 these reported sighting U-boats on 71 occasions and attacking them on 43. Air crews reported seventeen occasions when U-boats stayed on the surface and tried to fight off their attackers. During the month aircraft sank six U-boats in the Bay and caused severe damage to six more, for the loss of six aircraft shot down. Such a rate of exchange was overwhelmingly in favour of Coastal Command, for a patrol aircraft cost about one-fifth as much and carried one-eighth as many crew as a U-boat.

By the beginning of June almost every operational U-boat was fitted with anti-aircraft cannon, and *Admiral* Dönitz ordered a further change in tactics. Now the U-boats were to cross the Bay of Biscay on the surface by day in convoy. If an enemy aircraft attempted to attack them, their commanders had strict orders to remain on the surface and use their combined firepower to drive away or shoot down their assailants. After dark the U-boats were to submerge and continue their transit independently; at dawn they were to return to the surface, re-form and continue in convoy until they were clear of the Bay area.

When they were first tried in action, the group-sailing tactics enjoyed some success. A pair of boats reached Brest safely on 7 June after their patrol, as did another pair on the 11th. In the afternoon of the 12th, a patrolling aircraft sighted the first of the large groups to attempt to run the gauntlet—five U-boats on their way to the Atlantic. Darkness fell before an attack could be launched, and the U-boats continued their passage westward submerged. The following evening a Sunderland of No 228 Squadron regained contact with the group. Undeterred by the return fire, the crew carried out an accurate attack on *U564*, but their flying boat suffered mortal damage and shortly afterwards it crashed into the sea. The wounded *U564* was forced to abandon her patrol, and, escorted by one of the other boats, she headed for her base in France. On the following day a Whitley from No 10 Operational Training Unit found the pair and finished off the damaged boat; again the aircraft suffered damage in the encounter, however, and on the way home it was intercepted by German fighters and finished off. While all this was happening, the other three boats in the convoy escaped into the Atlantic.

The next two groups of U-boats which attempted to pass through the Bay on the surface both set sail on 12 June. One group, comprising three boats, crossed the Bay without loss after a running fight with aircraft, during which the German gunners inflicted damage on two of their attackers. The other group, comprising five boats, did not get off so lightly. Their adversaries were Mosquito fighters of

No 307 Squadron, which made repeated strafing runs with cannon. One of the British planes was damaged, but the rounds caused so many casualties among the crews of *U68* and *U155* that both boats had to abandon their patrols and return to base.

Having digested the lessons from these actions, *Admiral* Dönitz introduced yet another change of tactics. In the middle of June he ordered his U-boat groups to surface only by day, and then for the minimum time necessary for the boats to re-charge their batteries—about four hours in every twenty-four. This reduced the time spent on the surface, making it more difficult for enemy aircraft to find and attack the submarines. As a result of this change, in the final two weeks in June only one U-boat suffered damage from air attack in the Bay area.

The group-sailing tactics now being employed by the U-boats were not unlike those used by Allied merchant ships crossing the Atlantic. The counter-tactics devised by Coastal Command bore a striking resemblance to the 'wolf-pack' methods that the U-boats used with such effect against those Allied convoys. Three times a day, every day, a force of seven assorted patrol aircraft flew on parallel tracks over the transit routes used by the U-boats. If one of the aircraft located a U-boat group, it was to maintain contact out of reach of the return fire and report the position and composition of the enemy force by radio to headquarters. The other planes in the force could assemble over the U-boat group and deliver a concerted attack. The Allied aerial 'wolf-pack' tactics were an immediate success, and July 1943 was the most fruitful month of all for the Bay air patrols: eleven U-boats were sunk and three were seriously damaged, in exchange for six aircraft destroyed.

During this phase of the campaign every action had its unique features and it would be misleading to describe any one of them as 'typical'. However, the action that took place on 30 July was certainly one of the more dramatic and the most successful for the aircraft. That morning a Liberator of No 53 Squadron found a trio of U-boats—*U461* and *U462*, large submarine tankers equipped to refuel attack boats in mid-ocean, in company with *U504*—on the surface and heading west. The aircraft's radio report summoned six other aircraft to the scene—another Liberator, two Halifaxes, two Sunderlands and a Catalina.

A Halifax initiated the attack, making its bombing run from the relatively high altitude of 1,600ft to release three 600lb depth bombs; these weapons had cases stronger than those of normal depth charges, so that they would not break up on impact when released from higher altitudes. The additional altitude did not save the bomber from the U-boats' return fire, however, and it was forced to break off the action with a damaged elevator. The depth bombs fell wide. The second Halifax then attacked from 3,000ft, where it was relatively safe from the return fire, to release its stick of depth bombs. One of these weapons exploded close to *U462*, causing severe damage. Dark smoke issued from the conning tower, and about a quarter of an hour later the boat lost all speed, slid to a halt and began to settle in the water.

The other two U-boats circled protectively round the drifting craft, providing the opportunity for three of the aircraft to run in for a concerted attack at low altitude. The Liberator that made the initial sighting led the charge, accompanied by a Liberator of No 19 Squadron USAAF. Following some distance behind came a Sunderland from No 461 (Australian) Squadron. The Liberators encountered vigorous return fire, and both suffered damage and were forced to break off their attacks prematurely. But the presence of these planes had kept the German gunners busy long enough for the Sunderland to line up for an accurate attack on the undamaged tanker boat. Only at the last moment did the boat's guns begin traversing to meet the new threat, and by then it was too late. The flying boat's nose gunner loosed off a long and accurate burst which silenced the weapons. Then, his target defenceless, the Sunderland pilot released a stick of seven depth charges from 50ft and they exploded along the length of the boat. The submarine broke in two and sank almost immediately.

Probably rightly, the captain of *U504* decided that he could do nothing further to help his comrades and he took his boat down. The move was too late to save him or his craft, however. Since it had made contact with the enemy force, the Catalina had been directing a Royal Navy submarine hunting team of five sloops to the scene. The vessels arrived in time to dispatch *U462* with gunfire, then they carried out a sonar search for *U504* and sank her too. When the German naval records were examined after the war, it became clear that during the action there had been a remarkable coincidence of numbers: the submarine tanker *U461* had been sunk by Sunderland 'U' of No 461 Squadron.

August began in triumphant vein for the patrol aircraft, with the sinking of four more U-boats in the Bay area during the first two days. Then *Admiral* Dönitz decided that enough was enough. It was clear that the enemy had taken the measure of the group-sailing tactics, and he ordered his crews to cease using them. Those groups of boats that were committed to a transit of the Bay were to split up. The craft were to proceed singly, surfacing to recharge their batteries for as short a time as necessary and *only at night*. Four boats returning from patrol were told to hug the coast of neutral Spain, also surfacing only at night and only long enough to recharge their batteries.

The use of Spanish territorial waters provided the best answer to German submariners' problems, for the clutter of echoes from the land made it difficult to detect boats on radar. Soon afterwards a new type of radar warning receiver began to appear in U-boats, the *Naxos* equipment, which picked up microwave emissions from the ASV III and SCR-517 radars. The new receiver restored the technical balance in favour of the U-boats. But it had entered service too late, and other influences came to bear to nullify the German advantage.

Following a series of heavy defeats at the hands of the Allied convoy escorts, at the end of August Dönitz decided to suspend large-scale operations in that area. He needed to conserve his trained crews to man the new, high-performance U-boats he planned to introduce into service during the following year. The move reduced the transit of U-boats through the Bay of Biscay to a trickle. Although the air patrols continued with their previous intensity, between the end of the first week in August and the end of the 1943 they sank only five U-boats and damaged only one.

The Battle of the Bay began early in 1941, and the campaign finally ended when Allied ground forces neared the U-boat bases in France in the summer of 1944. The hardest-fought phase was during the fifteen-month period between the introduction of the Leigh Light in June 1942 and the withdrawal of the U-boats from the mid-Atlantic in August 1943. In that time the patrol aircraft sank 33 German and Italian submarines in the area, damaged 30 others and shared the destruction of one with surface ships.

CHAPTER EIGHT

The Regensburg Strike

*During the first seven months of 1943, the heavy bombers of the US Eighth Army
Air Force based in England penetrated progressively deeper into
Germany to deliver attacks. On 17 August its commander ordered the most ambi-
tious operation so far: a strike on the Messerschmitt aircraft factory at Regensburg in the extreme south of Germany, to be combined with another on the
ball-bearing production plant at Schweinfurt. The action that followed would lead
to a fundamental change in US strategic bombing policy.*

DURING JULY 1943 the Messerschmitt aircraft works at Regensburg in Bavaria delivered just under three hundred Bf 109 fighters to the *Luftwaffe*, making it
one of the largest of the four plants producing the type. Regensburg had always
been high on the list of targets earmarked for precision daylight attack. But the
risks involved in such a lengthy incursion into Germany were great: the factory
complex lay more than 500 miles from the nearest US bomber base in East Anglia, and 430 miles inside occupied Europe.

When the attack on Regensburg was being planned, that target became linked
with another of strategic importance that lay nearby—the ball-bearing production
centre at Schweinfurt, about 130 miles to the north-west. It was decided to launch
a twin-pronged thrust against both targets. Under the original plan, two raiding
forces, with a total of 376 B-17 Flying Fortresses, were to penetrate into Germany
together. At a point south of Frankfurt, the two rear divisions were to split away
from that in the lead, deliver their attack on Schweinfurt and return to England;
the remaining division, comprising 146 B-17s, was to continue on its south-east-
erly heading for Regensburg. After bombing, this force was to turn on to a
south-south-westerly heading over Austria and Italy, then over the Mediterranean
to Algeria in North Africa, where the bombers were to land. The purpose of the
stratagem was to avoid a long withdrawal flight over north-western Germany,
with possible heavy losses. Including formation assembly, the flight would take
eleven hours; even for the long-range version of the B-17, that would be close to
the limit of the aircraft's endurance.

P-47 Thunderbolt escort fighters were to cover the initial part of the bombers'
penetration, and the final part of the withdrawal of the Schweinfurt raiding force.
At this stage of the war, the escorts carried insufficient fuel to protect bombers
into Germany itself. The Royal Air Force was to contribute twenty squadrons of
Spitfires to support the operation, though the radius of action of these aircraft was
even more limited than that of the Thunderbolt. The 'bottom line' for the Regensburg attack force was that, in order to reach its target, it would have to fight its

way though 300 miles of hostile airspace after the last of the escorting fighters turned for home.

So much for the plan. Early on 17 August a thick layer of cloud lay over eastern England, which was forecast to thin out as the day progressed. Had the raiding forces taken off soon after dawn, as originally scheduled, there would have been a high risk of collision during formation assembly. Because of this, the attack plan was rescheduled. The Regensburg attack force was to take off 1½ hours later than planned (that was the maximum acceptable delay, since the bombers had to reach the unfamiliar airfields in Algeria before dusk). The larger Schweinfurt attack force faced no such constraint and had less far to go, so it was to delay its take-off by five hours to allow time for the skies over East Anglia to clear. Tactically, the change of plan was significant: it meant that the two attack forces were to penetrate into enemy territory separately and that each one in turn would face the full wrath of the German air defences.

At 10.05 a.m. the leading elements of the Regensburg attack force crossed the Dutch coast. Eight bombers had been forced to turn back for various reasons before reaching the coast, and the force now comprised 139 Flying Fortresses in three combat wing formations. Accompanying the bombers during the initial part of the penetration were a couple of dozen Thunderbolts of the 353rd Fighter Group.

As the bombers droned across Holland, three *Luftwaffe Gruppen*, each with about twenty fighters, were moving separately into position to deliver attacks.

BOEING B-17F FLYING FORTRESS

Role: Ten-seat, four-engine heavy bomber.

Power: Four Wright R-1820 Cyclone turbo-supercharged, 14-cylinder, air-cooled, radial engines each developing 1,200hp at take-off.

Armament: The bomb load depended on the distance to be flown. During the maximum-range attack on Regensburg, aircraft carried ten 500lb high-explosive bombs or a similar weight of incendiaries. The forward-firing defensive armament depended upon the modification state of the aircraft but comprised at least two Browning .3in machine guns (although some planes carried as many as four Browning .5in machine guns in that position on hand-held mountings). There were two Browning .5in machine guns in each of the powered turrets above and below the fuselage, two on a hand-held mounting in the tail, one in each waist position and one in the radio operator's position firing from above the fuselage.

Performance: Typical formation cruising speed (with bomb load) 180mph at 22,000ft; demonstrated operational range during the Regensburg mission (including aircraft assembling formation, flying in formation, operational fuel reserves and 5,000lb bomb load released near mid-point of flight) 1,500 miles.

Normal operational take-off weight: 48,720lb.

Dimensions: Span 103ft 9½in; length 74ft 8¾in; wing area 1,420 sq ft.

Date of first production B-17F: May 1942.

Note: B-17s taking part in the Regensburg mission were the extended-range version of the aircraft, with additional fuel cells in the outer wings (nicknamed 'Tokyo tanks').

The bomber formation was spread across twenty miles of sky and the small force of escorts could not cover every part of it. The Thunderbolts successfully drove off the Focke Wulf 190s of *II Gruppe* of *Jagdgeschwader 1*. But while the escorts were thus engaged, the two other *Gruppen*, *I* of *JG 26* with FW 190s and *III* of *JG 26* with Messerschmitt Bf 109s, each delivered a sharp head-on attack on part of the bomber formation.

Lieutenant-Colonel Beirne Lay, a staff officer at Headquarters Eighth Air Force, flew with the raiding force as a co-pilot in a B-17 of the 100th Bomb Group in order to gain first-hand experience of aerial combat. That he would certainly get, for the 100th was at the very rear of the formation in the most exposed position of all. Later Lay wrote a dramatic account of the air action, in which he described the initial encounter with the enemy:

> At 1017 hours, near Woensdrecht [in Holland], I saw the first flak blossom in our vicinity, light and inaccurate. A few minutes later two FW 190s appeared at one o'clock level and whizzed through the formation ahead of us in a frontal attack, nicking two B-17s in the wings and breaking away beneath us in half rolls. Smoke immediately trailed from both B-17s but they held their stations. As the fighters passed us at a high rate of closure, the guns of our group went into action. The pungent smell of burnt powder filled our cockpit and the B-17 trembled to the recoil of nose and ball-turret guns. I saw pieces fly off the wing of one of the fighters before they passed from view.

By the end of the encounter, two B-17s had been shot down and several damaged, in some cases so severely that they were forced to break formation and turn for home. Three Messerschmitts were shot down during the engagement.

Soon afterwards the 353rd Fighter Group was relieved by the 56th Fighter Group, and the latter, a more experienced unit, successfully blocked further attacks by enemy fighters on the main formation. The Thunderbolts could do nothing to protect the bombers against enemy flak, however, and two B-17s fell to this cause over Holland and others suffered damage. Unable to reach the main bomber formation, German fighters in the area concentrated their attentions on finishing off a couple of B-17s that had been forced out of formation and were returning to England alone. As the B-17s neared the German frontier, the Thunderbolts reached the limit of their radius of action and had to turn back.

Ahead of the Regensburg attack force lay a flight of more than 300 lonely miles to the target. The *Luftwaffe* fighter units based along the coastal strip had spent their force, however, and their aircraft were making for airfields in the area to refuel and re-arm. For the first time since the bombers crossed the coast, there was relative calm around their formation. Yet few of those on board the American bombers doubted that this was anything other than the lull before the storm.

Trailing the bombers like hungry jackals, taking care to keep outside of range of their guns, were a few Messerschmitt Bf 110 night fighters. The crews of these relatively slow and unwieldy radar-equipped planes had orders not to engage bombers in formation: their role was to finish off stragglers or any others that left the protection of the formation.

One night fighter took on the role of contact aircraft, maintaining a commentary on its position, course, altitude and composition. Beirne Lay had particular memories of that aircraft:

> I noticed an Me 110 sitting out of range on our right. He was to stay with us all the way to the target, apparently reporting our positions to fresh squadrons waiting for us down the road.

Lay's assessment was correct. By now it was clear to the German fighter controllers that the raiding force was heading for a target in the centre or the south of country, though its exact destination remained a matter of conjecture. The only regular day fighter unit in position to meet such a thrust was *Jagdgruppe 50*, the newly formed unit with 25 Bf 109s based at Wiesbaden/Erbenheim. Backing this unit were about a score of Bf 109s and FW 190s flown by instructors from fighter operational training units in the area, and more low-performance Bf 110 night fighters that could finish off stragglers.

The next action opened as the bombers passed Wiesbaden. One of the *Jagdgruppe 50* pilots, *Leutnant* Alfred Grislawski, later commented:

> We climbed and made perfect contact with the Boeings. It was my first view of an American formation. There were so many of them that we were all shaken to the marrow, both our small group of pilots from Russia and the young new pilots—the young ones a bit more than us I think. We started making frontal attacks on the right-hand-side formation; we went in in fours.

Knowing that these B-17s were about to bomb their homeland, the German pilots attacked with great determination. They also knew they had nothing to fear from enemy fighters, so they could afford to take their time positioning themselves for their firing runs and they could expend all of their ammunition against the bombers.

After delivering head-on attacks, the fighters turned around and made further attacks on the bombers from the rear. Much of the action was now concentrated around the embattled 100th Bomb Group at the rear of the formation. Beirne Lay wrote:

> Swinging their yellow noses around in a wide U-turn, a twelve-ship squadron of Me 109s came in from twelve to two o'clock in pairs and in fours, and the main event was on.
>
> A shining silver object sailed over our right wing. I recognised it as a main exit door. Seconds later, a dark object came hurtling through the formation, barely missing several props. It was a man, clasping his knees to his head, revolving like a diver in a triple somersault. I didn't see his chute open.
>
> A B-17 turned gradually out of the formation to the right, maintaining altitude. In a split second the B-17 completely disappeared in a brilliant explosion, from which the only remains were four small balls of fire, the fuel tanks, which were quickly consumed as they fell earthward.
>
> Our airplane was endangered by falling debris. Emergency hatches, exit doors, prematurely opened parachutes, bodies and assorted fragments of B-17s and Hun fighters breezed past us in the slipstream.

MESSERSCHMITT BF 109G-6

Role: Single-seat day fighter.

Power: One Daimler Benz DB 605 12-cylinder, liquid-cooled, in-line engine developing 1,475hp at take-off.

Armament: (Air defence role) Three Mauser MG 151 cannon, one firing through the propeller boss and one mounted under each wing; two Rheinmetall Borsig MG 131 13mm machine guns mounted above the engine.

Performance: Maximum speed 386mph at 22,650ft; climb to 18,700ft, 6min.

Normal operational take-off weight: 6,940lb.

Dimensions: Span 32ft 6½in; length 29ft 0½in; wing area 174 sq ft.

Date of first production Bf 109G-6: Late 1942.

I watched two fighters explode not far beneath, disappearing in sheets of orange flame, B-17s dropping out in every state of distress, from engines on fire to control surfaces shot away, friendly and enemy parachutes floating down and, on the green carpet far beneath us, numerous funeral pyres of smoke from fallen aircraft, marking our trail. The sight was fantastic: it surpassed fiction . . .

A B-17 of the Group ahead, with its right Tokyo tanks on fire, dropped back to about 200 feet above our right wing and stayed there while seven of the crew successively bailed out. Four went out of the bomb bay and executed delayed jumps, one bailed from the nose, opened his chute prematurely and nearly fouled the tail. Another went out the left-waist-gun opening, [and] delayed his chute opening for a safe interval. The tail gunner dropped out of his hatch, apparently pulling the ripcord before he was clear of the ship, and jerked him so hard that both his shoes came off. He hung limp in the harness, whereas the others had shown immediate signs of life after their chutes opened, shifting around in the harness. The B-17 then dropped back in a medium spiral and I did not see the pilots leave. I saw it just before it passed from view, several thousand feet below us, with its right wing a sheet of yellow flame.

Seven B-17s were shot down in rapid succession during this phase of the action. Two more suffered damage and were forced out of formation, to be finished off soon afterwards by German fighters. Of those nine bombers, six were from the 100th Bomb Group with which Lay was flying.

As the raiders passed east of Mannheim, the single-engine fighters began to run out of ammunition. One by one they broke away from the fight and the action fizzled out. Of the 139 Flying Fortresses that had crossed the Dutch coast, a total of fourteen had now been shot down, and in the case of several others the crews were struggling to keep their damaged planes in formation.

Few in the raiding force realized it, but in fact the defending fighter force had shot its bolt. The B-17s were now deeper inside Germany than they had ever been before, and had entered an area where there were no regular *Luftwaffe* day fighter units. For the final 25 minutes to the target, the bombers were unmolested, though a few Bf 110 night fighters remained ominously in position on the flanks and behind the raiders.

Because the US daylight bombers had never ventured near Regensburg before, the aircraft plant had only weak defences—a few newly built Bf 109s armed and kept on standby at the works airfield, to be flown by factory test pilots, and three batteries of 88mm anti-aircraft guns.

As the raiders neared Regensburg, they found the weather in the area perfect for an attack, with cloud-free skies and horizontal visibility 25 to 30 miles. At the designated Initial Point for the attack, 25 miles to the west of the target, the leading combat box moved into attack formation. The low and high squadrons moved into trail behind the lead squadron, to reduce the width of the formation for the bomb run. The leading unit, the 96th Bomb Group, arrived unscathed at the IP with all 21 of its B-17s.

Within each Bomb Group formation only four aircraft carried bomb sights, those of the leader, the deputy leader and the leaders of the high and the low squadrons. In the case of the three last, the sights were carried only as a back-up in case of losses. Provided he were still at the head of the formation and his equipment were serviceable, the bombardier in the lead aircraft aimed the bombs of the entire Group. Once the lead B-17 was established on its bomb run, its pilot engaged the autopilot and from then till bomb release the bombardier 'flew' the aircraft. The autopilot was linked electrically to the plane's Norden bomb sight, so that, each time the bombardier adjusted the sight to keep the aiming cross on the target, this fed corrections into the autopilot to steer the aircraft on the right path for an accurate attack.

For this raid the bomber crews had been briefed to attack from altitudes of between 17,000 and 20,000ft, depending on their position in the formation. That was less than the B-17's maximum attack altitude, to give improved bombing accuracy against this particularly important target. Captain John Latham was the lead bombardier for the 96th Bomb Group at the head of the raiding force. Later he commented:

> As lead bombardier I felt a great sense of responsibility because, if I missed the target, then all of the planes in my formation missed. When you have flown many hours and fought hard and lost many friends from fighters and anti-aircraft fire, it is extremely difficult to condone the failure of the one person upon whom the success of the entire effort depended.

The bombers attacked the target on a due easterly heading and Latham aimed his bombs at a point on the far (eastern) side of the target complex. Regensburg's few anti-aircraft batteries did their best to disrupt the attack, as did the few Messerschmitt fighters that had taken off from the airfield beside the factory. But these weak forces could do little to blunt the force of the bombardment.

When John Latham's B-17 reached the bomb-release point computed by the Norden bomb sight, a pair of electrical contacts snapped closed to release the plane's ten 500lb high-explosive bombs in rapid succession. The rest of the Group held tight formation on the lead aircraft during the bomb run, and when the latter's bombs were seen falling away, the rest of the B-17s in the formation released theirs. Using this method, bombs would be put down in a dense pattern on the ground, running back along a track from the leader's aiming point, the breadth of that pattern being the width of the formation at bomb release.

After bomb release, the pilot of the lead aircraft disengaged the autopilot and commenced a sweeping turn to the right, setting course for Algeria. As his bomber turned away, Latham moved to a side window to observe the results of his handiwork:

> It was just as though we had the conditions made to order and we saw what we hoped to see. Our bombs fell just on the leading edge of the target. It was perfect. We saw the rest of the Group's effort a split second later, moving across the target in a rapid series of bursts. Even from the height we were at, you could see, just momentarily, each bomb hitting the ground, either creating a hole in the ground or sending bricks flying, and then the whitish red of the explosion followed by a cloud of dust growing bigger and bigger and spreading across the target, with the flashes of further bombs continuing to be seen in the smoke and dust.

The lead bombardiers of the first three Bomb Groups to pass over the target were able to see the aiming points easily, and in each case their bomb patterns were extremely accurate. Then, as was so often the case when a large number of bombers attacked the same target, the clouds of dust thrown up by the explosions and smoke rising from the numerous fires began to drift over the aiming points, making them difficult to pick out. The later formations found conditions getting progressively more difficult, and two Bomb Groups, the 94th and the 385th, found visibility so bad that they were unable to release their weapons during their initial bomb runs and had to turn around and make second runs. The 122 bombers that reached the target took 22 minutes to complete their attack, that time being extended by the need for the two Bomb Groups to make second bomb runs.

Despite the problems with failing visibility, the B-17s laid accurate carpets of bombs over the factory complex. The plant area was hit hard and the raid killed about 400 workers and inflicted injuries on a similar number. After leaving the target, the B-17s continued south over the Alps. Two damaged B-17s left the formation and headed for the safety of neutral Switzerland, the first of these aircraft to land there. Describing the 1,000-mile flight from the target to the recovery airfields in Africa, Beirne Lay later wrote:

> The rest of the trip was a marked anticlimax. A few more fighters pecked at us on the way to the Alps. A town in the Brenner Pass tossed up a lone burst of futile flak. We circled over Lake Garda [in northern Italy] long enough to give the cripples [damaged aircraft] a chance to join the family, and we were on our way toward the Mediterranean in a gradual descent. The prospect of ditching as we approached North Africa, short of fuel, and the sight of other B-17s falling into the drink, seemed trivial matters after the vicious nightmare of the long trip across southern Germany. We felt the reaction of men who had not expected to see another sunset.

During the flight from the target a further seven B-17s went down, all of them after having suffered battle damage earlier. In several cases the aircraft had lost fuel from holed tanks and were forced to put down short of their destination.

Of the 146 heavy bombers that had set out from England earlier in the day, 139 had penetrated occupied Europe; and of those, 115 succeeded in landing at airfields in friendly territory. As was often the case in a hard-fought air action of this kind, the losses were not distributed evenly throughout the force. The unit that took the heaviest battering was the 100th Bomb Group, the one with which Beirne Lay flew, in the most exposed position at the rear of the force: of its 21 B-17s, nine were shot down. In contrast, the 96th Bomb Group, which led the raid, suffered no losses at all, and two other units, the 94th and the 388th Bomb Groups, lost only one aircraft each. The air–sea rescue services of both sides turned in an exemplary performance and, miraculously, every man on board the five B-17s of the Regensburg attack force that ditched in the North Sea or the Mediterranean was picked up safely.

In the course of the action, the Regensburg attack force lost 24 B-17s, 16.4 per cent of the force. But that was not the final cost of the raid. A week later 85 of those aircraft took off from Algeria to return to England, attacking an airfield in western France on the way. The rest of the B-17s that landed in Algeria had been damaged too severely to be repaired in time at the poorly equipped landing grounds there. Some of the damaged planes would later be repaired and would return in ones and twos. But in the short term the attack on Regensburg deprived the Eighth Air Force of 61 bombers—uncomfortably close to half of those committed to the venture. During the mission the B-17s' gunners claimed to have destroyed 140 German fighters in air-to-air combat. It was a massive exaggeration, with every fighter that was shot down being claimed several times: from an examination of *Luftwaffe* records, it is clear that fewer than ten German fighters were shot down while engaging the Regensburg attack force.

As has been said, the bombing of the Regensburg aircraft production complex was both accurate and concentrated: it was a fine example of the precision air attack theories then being pushed hard by the US Army Air Forces. Reconnaissance photographs taken after the raid showed a high proportion of the buildings at the plant to be wrecked or burnt-out. Viewing the damage, Allied intelligence officers assessed that production would be halted for several weeks and greatly reduced for several months after that. It was an over-optimistic prognosis.

Once the debris had been cleared away, company officials found that most of machine tools and production jigs at the plant had survived intact. The buildings were repaired or, where this was not possible, the machine tools were quickly re-sited. Production resumed, and in September 1943, the month following the attack, the Regensburg factory delivered nearly eighty Bf 109s to the *Luftwaffe*. In October there were 163 and in November 205. By December, monthly production reached 270, exactly the same as it had been before the attack. The sag in Bf 109 production at the plant amounted to about 400 aircraft, or about 12 per cent of those that would have been built during a four-month period had the raid not taken place. Although the attack administered a heavy blow, it was one from which the *Luftwaffe* would soon recover.

In truth, the 272 tons of bombs that the B-17s laid across the target was insufficient to 'destroy' a factory complex the size of that at Regensburg. Moreover, the

500lb high-explosive bomb, the largest weapon used during the raid, was insufficiently powerful to cause serious damage among machine tools, even if it exploded on the building housing them. As the Allies would learn when they examined the German records after the war, in order to halt production at such a plant, it would be necessary to mount repeated attacks in similar strength at regular intervals.

* * *

To round off this account of the attack on Regensburg, we need to look briefly at the fate of the attack on Schweinfurt by 230 Flying Fortresses later on 17 August 1943. These raiders also suffered heavily at the hands of the German fighters, losing 36 bombers. Thus, of the 376 Flying Fortresses that set out from England that day to bomb the two important targets, a total of sixty were destroyed in action.

Both sides learned important lessons from the day's actions. The US Army Air Forces learned that the crossfire from a large formation of heavy bombers could not prevent the latter from suffering unacceptably heavy losses during deep-penetration attacks on Germany. The solution was give a high priority to the production of long-range escort fighter types, notably the P-51B Mustang. When the latter became available in quantity early the following year, it would have a decisive impact on the course of the strategic bombing offensive.

For the German High Command there were other, quite different lessons. The first was the need to pull back more fighter units from the Eastern and the Mediterranean Fronts, to buttress those defending the homeland. This would be done. To allow the formation of more fighter units, the production of these aircraft was stepped up, at the expense of bombers and other types. Moves were made to augment the firepower of home defence fighters, to increase their effectiveness in the bomber-destroyer role. Simultaneously, work began to disperse the production of aircraft and aero-engines among many scores of small factories scattered across the country, instead of concentrating it at a relatively few large plants that were known to the enemy and therefore liable to attack. And, as a long-term solution to defeat the bombers, the *Luftwaffe* poured resources into getting the revolutionary new Messerschmitt Me 262 jet fighter into production and first-line service as rapidly as possible. The degree of success that attended their efforts with the last of these is described in Chapter 12, 'The Jets Get Their Chance'.

THE RISE AND DEMISE OF THE STUKA

Above: Junkers Ju 87 dive-bombers of *Sturz-kampfgeschwader 77* returning from a mission. (Schmidt)

Right: A view over the nose of a Ju 87 during a near-vertical dive on a fortified position. (Schmidt)

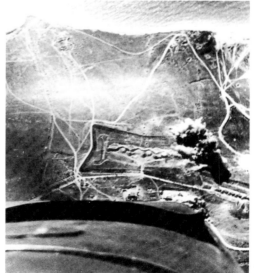

Left: A Ju 87 makes its last dive after being shot down by RAF fighters near Chichester on 18 August 1940.
Below: Snow-camouflaged Junkers Ju 87 dive-bombers of *I Gruppe, Sturzkampf-geschwader 5* operating on the Northern Front in Russia. (Schmidt)

Right: *Hauptmann* Helmut Mahlke flew the Ju 87 with *Trägergruppe 186* during the campaign in France, and his comments are quoted in the account. (Mahlke)

LOW ALTITUDE ATTACK
Below right: *Hauptmann* Joachim Roth led the low-altitude attack on Kenley on 18 August 1940. (Raab)

Left, top: Do 17s of the 9th *Staffel* of *Kampfgeschwader 76* heading towards the coast of England near Beachy Head on their way to attack Kenley on 18 August 1940.

Left, centre: Roth's aircraft, pictured at Leaves Green after it crash-landed.

COUNTERING THE NIGHT BOMBER

Left, bottom: A Heinkel He 111, carrying two 2,200lb bombs under the fuselage, takes off for an attack on Great Britain.

Right: Hans-George Bätcher at the controls of an He 111, pictured later in the war when he held the rank of *Oberst* (Colonel). (Bätcher)

Below right: The Bristol Beaufighter, the first effective night fighter type to enter service with the RAF, which came close to shooting down Bätcher during the early morning darkness of 9 July 1941.

BATTLE OF THE CORAL SEA

Above: A Mitsubishi B5N 'Kate' with a Type 91 torpedo under the fuselage, taking off from a Japanese aircraft carrier. The Type 91 was considerably more effective than its American counterpart and it played an important part in assisting the Japanese advance during the early part of the war in the Pacific. (USN)

Below: The Grumman F4F Wildcat was the only effective fighter type operated by the US Navy when the Pacific War began. (USN)

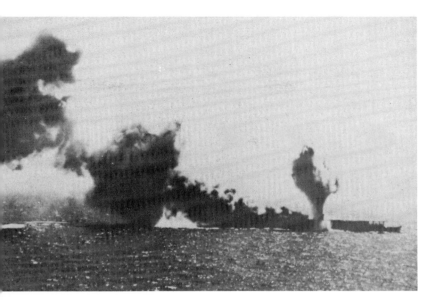

Above: The Japanese light carrier *Shoho* under heavy attack and taking a torpedo hit amidships, shortly before she capsized and sank. (USN)
Below: The US Navy carrier *Lexington*, abandoned, on fire and listing, after fumes from a leaking aviation fuel tank ignited, causing a major explosion. (USN)

BATTLE OF THE BAY

Left: A Vickers Wellington maritime patrol aircraft, with a Leigh Light extended beneath the rear fuselage and a radome for ASV Mk III radar under the nose. (Leigh)

Below left: A British submarine illuminated by a Leigh Light during early trials with the device. (Leigh)

Right: To protect themselves against air attack, U-boats were fitted with batteries of anti-aircraft weapons. This was the installation on *U802*—three mountings with eight 20mm cannon. (Selinger)

Below: A U-boat in the Bay under attack from a US Navy Liberator. (US Navy)

THE REGENSBURG STRIKE
Above: A Boeing B-17F Flying Fortress of the 96th Bomb Group releasing its load of ten 500lb bombs over the target. This unit led the attack on Regensburg on 17 August 1943. (USAF)

RECONNAISSANCE TO BERLIN
Left: Major Walt Weitner, commander of the 14th Photo Squadron, 7th Photographic Reconnaissance Group, US Eighth Air Force, who flew a Spitfire to Berlin on 6 March 1944 to photograph the target after the first large-scale attack on the city by US heavy bombers. (Weitner)

THE NUREMBERG DISASTER

Above: A Lancaster of No 463 (Australian) Squadron about to be loaded with two 4,000lb high-explosive bombs and twelve containers of incendiaries. (Via Garbett)

Left, upper: A Messerschmitt Bf 110G—the mainstay of the *Luftwaffe*'s night fighter force during the action of the night of 30/31 March 1944—running up on the ground. Note the large aerial array on the nose, belonging to the *SN-2* radar.

Left, lower: The wreckage of a Halifax of No 427 (Canadian) Squadron shot down over occupied Europe. This unit lost three aircraft during the attack on Nuremberg.

THE DAY OF THE STURMGRUPPE

Above: A Focke Wulf FW 190A-8 *Sturmbock* aircraft, fitted with additional armour and two 30mm heavy cannon for close-range attacks on US bombers. (Romm)

Left, upper: *Leutnant* Walther Hagenah, one of the first pilots to volunteer to serve with a *Sturmgruppe*. (Hagenah)

Left, lower: A B-24 Liberator in severe trouble after being hit from close range during a *Sturmgruppe* attack.

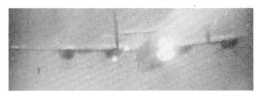

THE JETS GET THEIR CHANCE

Above: A line-up of Messerschmitt Me 262 fighters at Lechfeld in the summer of 1944.

Right, upper: *General-leutnant* Adolf Galland, who at the end of the war commanded the élite Me 262 unit *Jagdverband 44*, is seen here during a meeting with Adolf Hitler. Standing in the *Führer*'s shadow is *Generalfeldmarschal* Erhard Milch, who was censured for failing to ensure that the jet plane was modified to carry out the fighter-bomber role.

Right, lower: North American Mustang escort fighters—three P-51Ds with bubble canopies nearest the camera and a P-51C furthest away—belonging to the 361st Fighter Group. A pilot from this unit, Lieutenant Urban Drew, shot down the first two Me 262s to be lost in combat. The Mustangs, with their long range and high perform-ance, were a constant problem for the German jet fighter pilots. (USAF)

FURBALL OVER HAI DUONG

Left, top: McDonnell F-4J Phantom No 100, the aircraft in which Lieutenant-Commander Randy Cunningham and back-seater Willie Driscoll shot down three MiG fighters on 10 May 1972 before they were themselves shot down by a surface-to-air missile. (USN)

Left, centre: North Vietnamese fighter pilots run to their MiG-17s.

LOW DRAMA IN FRONT OF SAN CARLOS

Left, bottom: A pair of Sea Harriers of No 801 Squadron return to HMS *Invincible* after an air defence mission over the Falklands.

Right, top: Commander 'Sharkey' Ward led No 801 Squadron during the Falklands conflict and shot down two Argentine aircraft during the action on 21 May 1982. (Ward)

Right, centre: A low-level attack on shipping in San Carlos Water, by a Dagger fighter-bomber of *Grupo 6* of the Argentine Air Force. (Dibb)

THE EPIC OF 'BRAVO NOVEMBER'

Right, bottom: 'Bravo November', the only RAF Chinook medium-lift helicopter to reach the Falklands during the conflict, delivers stores to the aircraft carrier HMS *Hermes*.

NIGHT PRECISION ATTACK

Right, upper: A General Dynamics F-111F of the 48th Tactical Fighter Wing, carrying four 2,000lb laser-guided bombs. (USAF)
Right, lower: Colonel Tom Lennon USAF, commander of the 48th TFW during the war in the Persian Gulf. (USAF)

ST VALENTINE'S DAY SHOOT-DOWN

Below: Safely home: Rupert Clark pictured in front of a Tornado of No 15 Squadron, after his return from captivity in Iraq. (RAF Leuchars)

CHAPTER NINE

Reconnaissance to Berlin

This chapter looks at an important aspect of air warfare—photographic reconnaissance. Flying a long-range reconnaissance mission in wartime requires special skills and a special kind of bravery. In the Second World War, the aircraft operated alone, and usually without armament, at extremes of altitude, speed and often range, penetrating deep into hostile territory to photograph their targets. Once the pictures had been taken, the mission was only half complete, for the finest photographs were of no use unless they could be brought back for processing and interpretation to extract the necessary intelligence.

HARSH EXPERIENCE has shown that, in war, it was usually much easier for reconnaissance aircraft to avoid the enemy defences than attempt to fight their way through them. For that reason, most specialized reconnaissance aircraft are stripped of armament, trading weight and drag for improvements in speed, altitude and range performance. Reconnaissance crews faced a range of foes, quite apart from the fighters and anti-aircraft guns of their human adversary. There was the psychological effect of being alone, deep in enemy territory, with little or no chance of receiving help in an emergency. There was the need to depend on the near-perfect functioning of a flying machine, and the knowledge that even a minor failure could result in death or a long stretch in a prisoner-of-war camp. There was the insidious enemy of boredom which, sometimes assisted by mind-numbing cold at high altitude, could reduce a man's concentration to a point that might be fatal if a sudden attack developed. Also, on maximum-range flights, there was the ever-present danger of running out of fuel if the pilot failed to use this precious commodity frugally or if, to avoid enemy fighters, he flew for too long at full throttle. Set against all of this, those that flew reconnaissance missions were regarded as a highly professional élite: they alone were able to play a recognizably important part in war without indulging in the grim business of slaughter.

Aerial reconnaissance missions take several forms. This account describes a post-strike reconnaissance mission, whose purpose was to provide photographs from which intelligence officers determined the damage inflicted on the target. After a strike, an air commander needed to know as soon as possible whether it had been successful, or if a follow-up attack were needed. Because the enemy would often expect the post-strike reconnaissance aircraft to follow a heavy attack, and arrange a suitable reception, this type of mission was potentially the most dangerous of all.

* * *

SUPERMARINE SPITFIRE PR Mk XI

Role: Single-seat, long-range, photographic reconnaissance aircraft.
Power: One Rolls-Royce Merlin 63 12-cylinder, liquid-cooled, in-line engine developing 1,760hp at take-off.
Armament: None carried. Military load during the mission described comprised two F.52 cameras (with 36in focal length lenses) fitted in the rear fuselage.
Performance: Maximum speed 417mph at 24,000ft; maximum operational radius of action (carrying a 90-gallon drop tank) 565 miles.
Normal operational take-off weight: 8,519lb.
Dimensions: Span 36ft 10in; length 31ft 1in; wing area 242 sq ft.
Date of first production Spitfire XI: November 1942.

On 6 March 1944 the US Eighth Air Force mounted the first of many large-scale attacks on Berlin. At 1.30 p.m., when the attack was at its climax, Major Walt Weitner eased his Spitfire off the ground at Bradwell Bay near Clacton and turned on to an easterly heading. Weitner commanded the 14th Photo Squadron, 7th Photographic Reconnaissance Group, a Eighth Air Force unit based at Mount Farm near Oxford which operated a mix of Lightnings and Spitfires modified for the long-range photographic-reconnaissance role.

Weitner's aircraft was a Spitfire PR Mk XI appropriately named 'High Lady'. Stripped of its armament, and with a pair of long focal length cameras installed in the rear fuselage, the much-modified fighter was a flying fuel tank. Almost the entire leading edge of both wings had been redesigned to form a large integral tank holding 132 gallons of high-octane petrol. With the 84 gallons in the main tanks in front of the cockpit, and a further 90 in the 'slipper' drop tank mounted under the fuselage, the aircraft carried 306 gallons of fuel. That was more than *three times* the fuel load carried by the early fighter versions of the aircraft.

The flight was planned to last over four hours, most of the time spent at high altitude, and Weitner wore several layers of clothing to keep out the cold. With all of this, plus a parachute, dinghy, life jacket and oxygen mask, the narrow confines of the Spitfire cockpit were no place for the claustrophobic.

Weitner took a direct route to the German capital, heading almost due east over the North Sea towards Holland. Just over half an hour after take-off, he passed his first check-point, The Hague, at 39,000ft. Below him there was five-tenths cloud cover, and he could make out the outline of the Zuider Zee to his left. He later recalled:

> The Spitfire was easy to handle at very high altitude. This one was well trimmed and stayed pretty level. One had always to have hold of the stick, but it needed hardly any pressure. In the reconnaissance business you do not fly straight and level for long: you are continually banking to search the sky all around for enemy fighters and check the navigation.

Outside the cockpit the temperature was around –60F. The thick layers of clothing kept most of his body warm, but nothing could prevent Weitner's extremities, his feet and his hands, from the numbing cold. From time to time he clapped his hands and stamped his feet on the cockpit floor to get the blood circulating again.

The flight at high altitude brought another problem: during its passage through the cold air, the Spitfire left behind a highly visible white condensation trail. Had Weitner wished to draw attention to his presence, there was hardly a better way of doing it, but the realities of the situation forced him to take a calculated risk:

> I could have avoided [the trail] by descending below 22,000 feet, but I did not think that was the thing to do on a deep penetration like this. I thought the best bet was to cruise near to the ceiling of a Messerschmitt 109; then, if I had to go up, I had a little margin of altitude I could use. The Germans must have known I was up there, but nobody was paying any attention to me.

Weitner thought that if enemy fighters climbed to high altitude after him, they too would leave condensation trails, and he would get plenty of warning of their approach.

As the Spitfire passed over Hanover the skies were clear, and Weitner switched on his cameras as he passed over the city. He noticed several condensation trails ahead at about his level, but the aircraft were moving on an easterly heading away from him. The reason for the defenders' present lack of interest in the lone Spitfire was not difficult to fathom: that afternoon almost every available German fighter in the area was battling against the huge force of bombers and their escorts now heading back to England.

As the air battle moved to the west and the Spitfire got closer to Berlin, the *Luftwaffe* finally reacted to the lone intruder. A glance in the rear-view mirrors in the canopy side-blisters revealed three enemy fighters holding formation on the Spitfire, 1,500yds behind and slightly below. All three aircraft were leaving condensation trails.

The arrival of the enemy fighters came at a bad time for the American pilot, forcing him to take another calculated risk. At this time his engine was running on the slipper tank, and from his calculations—which gave only a rough guide—he knew that the tank was nearly empty. If it ran dry, his first indication would be when the engine started to splutter—which might leave him without power at a critical point in the chase. He could switch to one of the internal tanks and release the drop tank, but to complete the mission he needed to use all the fuel that he had. If he released the drop tank, it would mess up his fuel calculations, and he might have to abandon the mission short of the target. Another alternative, to switch to one of the internal tanks, hold on to the slipper tank and use that fuel later, he rejected because the latter might not resume feeding. Weighing up the situation, Weitner decided to try to outrun the enemy fighters using the remaining fuel in the drop tank and hope that it held out long enough. He pushed the throttle as far forward as it would go without selecting emergency power, to pick up speed. Then he eased up the nose and began a shallow climb. As he did so, he kept one hand on the tank selector switch, ready to shift to one of the wing tanks when the engine faltered:

[83]

As I climbed through 40,000 feet I could see that the German fighters behind me had split: one went on my right and two on my left, to box me in. And at that moment the engine coughed. I immediately selected internal fuel and the engine caught right away. At 41,500 feet I levelled off and my indicated airspeed increased to 178mph [true airspeed about 360mph]. Gradually the German fighters began to fall back and finally the last slid from view.

Had the enemy planes got closer, Weitner could have pushed his throttle 'through the gate' to get full emergency boost to outrun his pursuers. But that would have increased fuel consumption greatly and he regarded it as a measure of last resort.

The enemy fighters that chased the Spitfire were almost certainly Messerschmitt Bf 109Gs specially fitted with nitrous oxide power-boosting to give an improved performance at high altitude. Probably the pursuers belonged to *I Gruppe* of *Jagdgeschwader 3*, based at Burg to the west of Berlin, one of the units that specialized in such interceptions.

When the enemy fighters passed out of sight, the Spitfire was getting near to the enemy capital. Maintaining a wary eye for other Messerschmitts trying to sneak up on him from behind, Weitner prepared to make his first photographic run over the city. Although he could see clearly the huge expanse of Lake Mueritz, some 50 miles to the north of Berlin, because of the smoke and industrial haze he still could not see the city itself. The Spitfire had no pressurized cabin, and to reduce the risk of decompression sickness Weitner did not want to remain at maximum altitude for longer than necessary. He eased the aircraft into a slow descent to 38,000ft and suddenly he caught sight of the sprawling city laid out beneath him, with the sun glinting off the red brick and tile houses.

Weitner decided to make his first photographic run from almost due north, down wind, to get a good line of photos without drifting off the target. He banked the Spitfire steeply and aligned himself on the string of lakes he was using as a check-point, carefully levelled the aircraft using the artificial horizon and then switched on the cameras.

The Spitfire carried two F.52 cameras mounted almost vertically in the rear fuselage, each with a 36in focal length lens. The cameras were splayed out sideways, giving a slight overlap in cover. At five-second intervals, the camera shutters opened and closed, to photograph a three-mile wide strip of ground beneath the aircraft. Accurate flying was essential during a photographic run; even a small amount of bank could cause gaps in the cover. During each five-second interval between successive pairs of photographs, Weitner made a painstaking check of his flight path and corrected it where necessary.

His orders were to photograph the targets bombed by the American heavy bombers, and to assist him he had aerial photographs of the city with the targets marked on them. But he could see pillars of smoke rising from other places and decided to photograph those also:

The whole time I kept checking the sky behind my tail, as I expected further interference from the enemy fighters. But none showed up. There was some flak—I could see the smoke bursts mushrooming—but none of it was close. I spent about

25 minutes over Berlin, during which I made runs from different directions and took about 70 photographs. Then a solid layer of cloud began moving over the city from the east, and as fuel was beginning to run low I set a course of 297 degrees for home.

Over Holland on the way home, the Spitfire pilot encountered a further problem with his fuel. The standard procedure was to use the fuel in the drop tank first; then that in the tanks in the wings, changing from one side to the other at fifteen-minute intervals to maintain the lateral trim; then the fuel in the lower main tank; and, last of all, that in the upper main tank. As the Merlin used the last of the fuel in the wing tanks, it coughed briefly, then resumed its even roar as Weitner selected the lower main tank. A glance at the fuel gauge caused the pilot's heart to miss a beat: the needle was jammed hard against the zero mark. If that reading was correct, the tank had been leaking and it would be almost empty, and there was insufficient fuel to regain friendly territory. The more palatable answer was that the tank was full but the fuel gauge had frozen up. Only time would tell which answer was correct.

Weitner made a few quick calculations which proved to his satisfaction that the main tanks had to be full. Any nagging fears were put to rest when the bank of cloud covering the English coast came within gliding distance. He began a slow descent from 38,000ft and soon after he crossed the coast of Essex the fuel gauge jerked into life showing a reading of 20 gallons.

Weitner had intended to land at one of the airfields near to the coast to refuel, but with so much altitude in hand he knew he could fly straight to his base at Mount Farm. Speed was of the essence in delivering the precious films for processing, and by continuing straight to his base he could save nearly an hour in getting the pictures into the hands of the interpreters.

'High Lady' landed at its base after a flight of 4 hours 18 minutes, and ran out of fuel a few yards short of its dispersal point. Walt Weitner pulled on the parking brake, slid back his canopy, undid his straps and climbed stiffly out of the cockpit. For the reconnaissance pilot it had been a successful ending to a rather routine mission.

CHAPTER TEN

The Nuremberg Disaster

In parallel with the American daylight bombing attacks on Germany, the Royal Air Force mounted attacks in strength by night. In the spring of 1944, following the introduction of new electronic detection equipment and a new airborne radar, the German night-fighter force reached the peak of its effectiveness. RAF night bombers engaged in deep-penetration attacks against targets in Germany began to suffer increasingly severe losses, until this phase of the battle reached its climax on the night of 30/31 March 1944.

AT 9.16 P.M. in the evening of 30 March 1944, the first of 782 Lancaster and Halifax four-engine bombers began taking off from their bases in eastern England. The target for the maximum-effort attack was the city of Nuremberg in southern Germany, an important centre for war production. Within its limits lay the huge Machninenfabrik Augsburg-Nürnberg plant producing diesel engines for tanks and U-boats, the Siemens plant turning out electrical equipment for the Navy and the Zundapp motor works building vehicles for the Army.

After take-off, each aircraft climbed in a spiral to an assigned altitude above 10,000ft, then set course for the force assembly point over the North Sea. Initially the bombers flew with their navigation lights on to lessen the risk of collision, but as they neared the Dutch coast the lights were extinguished and from then on each bomber crew was on its own.

Some accounts have likened the 'bomber stream' tactic employed by RAF night bombers to a loose formation, but such a description is grossly misleading. Crews were briefed to follow the same route and adhere to timing points along it, but the accuracy with which aircraft followed these depended on the skill and good fortune of individual navigators. As a result there was a natural tendency for a force of night bombers to spread itself out over a wide area. During the Nuremberg mission the raiders were divided into six separate waves which were to follow each other, snake-like, through a succession of turning points.

The plan called for the raiding force to pass through the target in a seventeen-minute period, which meant that, at the bombers' 220mph still-air cruising speed, the stream was to occupy a strip of sky 64 miles long and one mile (5,000ft) deep. Given the dispersion that usually occurred during night raids, in good conditions the bomber stream would be about ten miles wide. Even under ideal conditions, however, the density of aircraft within that 640 cubic miles of airspace was extremely low. If the bottom of this page can be taken to represent a distance of one mile, a single heavy bomber to that scale would be roughly the size of this letter 'T'. At the centre of a well-concentrated bomber stream there would be, on average, just two 'T'-size aircraft within the area represented by this page; if it were less well concentrated, there would be on average only one 'T' flying in that volume of sky.

Despite this relatively low density of aircraft, the bomber-stream tactic caused severe problems for the German night air defences. The bombers would pass any point on the route at an average of 46 per minute. That was sufficient to saturate the defending gun and searchlight defences and present far more targets than they could possibly engage. A concentrated stream was usually difficult for a night fighter crew to locate, though when a night fighter did get into the stream it sometimes caused considerable mayhem.

Shortly before 11 p.m., as the leading raiders were crossing the North Sea, they came into the view of German early-warning radar stations on the coasts of Belgium and Holland. Soon afterwards the first electronic jamming appeared on the radar screens, and this became increasingly severe as the night wore on.

Well before the vanguard of the raiding force reached the Dutch coast, the German fighter controllers had ordered their immediate-readiness aircraft to scramble. From their point of view, it was important to assemble a sizeable force of night fighters over western Germany as soon as possible after the incoming raid was detected. The cruising speed of the Messerschmitt Bf 110 and Junkers Ju 88 night fighters was little faster than that of the bombers they were expected to engage. As yet the raiders' target was unknown, but if it were in the west that could cause problems: the distance from the fighter bases in Denmark or near Berlin to the Ruhr was about the same as that from the bomber bases in Cambridgeshire to the German industrial area.

As the defending night fighters were taking off, the British radio-jamming organization made its presence felt. High-powered transmitters located in England and others carried by the bombers radiated a raucous cacophony on the German fighter radio channels. The *Luftwaffe* night fighter force war diarist noted:

Korps VHF [radio] jammed by bell sounds. R/T traffic hardly possible, jamming of *Korps* HF by quotations from *Führer*'s speeches. *Korps* alternative frequency strongly jammed.

AVRO LANCASTER Mk I

Role: Seven-seat heavy bomber.

Power: Four Rolls-Royce Merlin 24 12-cylinder, liquid-cooled in-line engines each developing 1,640hp at take-off.

Armament: (Offensive) During the attack on Nuremberg, a distant target, these aircraft carried a bomb load of around 9,000lb, the exact weight depending upon the mix of weapons carried; (defensive) eight Browning .303in machine guns, two each in the nose and mid-upper turrets and four in the tail.

Performance: Maximum speed 287mph at 11,500ft; normal cruising speed 220mph at 20,000ft; service ceiling 24,500ft.

Normal operational take-off weight: 68,000lb.

Dimensions: Span 102ft; length 69ft 6in; wing area 1,297 sq ft.

Date of first production Lancaster I: October 1941.

The electronic battle was not to be one-sided, however. The defenders were also well equipped in this regard, and they possessed systems whose existence was unknown to Bomber Command. The *Luftwaffe*'s raid-tracking service had developed to a fine art the technique of plotting the movement of bombers from their electronic emissions. The culprit radars were the H2S ground-mapping equipment and the 'Monica' tail-warning radar, both of which radiated distinctive signals that could be picked up from great ranges. The Germans had established a network of ground direction-finding stations across northern Europe to locate the sources of the emissions by triangulation. *Naxburg* receivers tracked the movements of H2S aircraft and *Korfu* receivers followed those transmitting with 'Monica'; furthermore, *Naxos* and *Flensburg* receivers fitted to some German night fighters enabled them to home on, respectively, the two types of radar emission (the airborne *Naxos* equipment was a variant of the device carried by U-boats, mentioned in Chapter 7).

In the battle now unfolding, the information from the new German devices would be valuable on four counts. First, because the H2S and 'Monica' signals emanated only from RAF aircraft, the sources were obviously and unambiguously hostile (with radar detection, identification was often a problem). Second, the German receivers were unjammable—unless the RAF adopted the irrational course of jamming its own radars. Third, the H2S radiations gave a clear indication of the whereabouts of the Pathfinder aircraft that led each wave of the raiding force to the target. And fourth, because they were passive devices, the receivers emitted no tell-tale radiations that would betray their existence.

The German night fighters carried a further new item of electronic equipment that would have an significant effect on the night's action—the *SN-2* airborne interception radar. The earlier *Lichtenstein* set had been rendered virtually useless by the 'Window' metal foil strips dropped by RAF bombers. The *SN-2* that replaced it operated on a longer wavelength and was relatively immune to the 'Window' then in use.

Shortly after midnight, the leading bombers crossed the Belgian/German frontier. Their crews found the weather far from ideal for a deep-penetration attack into enemy territory. Instead of the forecast cloud cover during the long approach flight to the target, they found the skies clear at the bombers' altitudes. Moreover, instead of the forecast wind of 60kts from the north-west, on their tails, the actual wind was variable in strength and more from the west. The more skilful navigators discovered the discrepancy relatively quickly and made the necessary corrections, but others took much longer to do so. As a result the force became spread out over a stretch of sky more than 120 miles long and 40 miles wide—more than four times the planned area.

As if that were not bad enough, a further quirk of the weather sealed the fate of many of the bomber crews heading into Germany. After high-octane petrol was burned in the bombers' engines, the residue emerged from the exhausts as steam, which normally dispersed without causing any problem. On this unusually cold night, however, the vapour condensed to form white trails at the raiders' altitudes of around 20,000ft. Lit by the half-full moon, the trails took on a phosphorescent quality that could be seen from great distances. Thus the bombers were shorn of the cloak of invisibility upon which their survival depended.

From his headquarters bunker at Deelen in Holland, *Generalmajor* Walter Grabmann, commanding *Jagddivision 3*, ordered the night fighters to assemble over radio beacon 'Ida' near Bonn. The usual tactic was to hold the fighters over the beacon until the bombers' route became clear, then have them head out on a set bearing until they made contact with the bomber stream. On this night it soon became obvious to the German commander that no further directions were necessary: many of the bombers in the stream, made diffuse by the wind speed and direction being different from what were forecast, were about to pass over 'Ida'.

Thanks to the *Naxburg* and *Korfu* ground receiving stations, the defenders had no difficulty in distinguishing the RAF feint attack forces from the main body of raiders. The German war diarist noted:

> Assembly, leaving England and approach could be followed correctly by *Rotterdam* bearings [*Rotterdam* was the German code-name for H2S]. Feint attacks on Cologne, Frankfurt and Kassel by Mosquitos appeared quite clearly, as the Mosquitos were flying without *Rotterdam*.

As the bombers passed over 'Ida', the radar operators in the orbiting night fighters made contact and guided their pilots on to individual bombers. As they closed on the enemy, the German crews had an important duty to perform before they went into action: they had to broadcast their position and the bombers' heading, to assist the *Luftwaffe* ground controllers to direct yet more fighters into the bomber stream. Soon the ether was thick with '*Pauke!*' calls, followed by position reports and headings. '*Pauke!*', the *Luftwaffe* equivalent of the RAF's 'Tally Ho!', meant that the fighter had made contact with the enemy and was about to engage.

Thus began a running battle that was to last for more than 200 miles across Germany. As well as the night fighters joining the bomber stream, a small number of Ju 88s from a special illuminating unit released parachute flares to mark its position. The flares were visible from scores of miles away, and from all over Germany night fighters converged on the area like moths to a flame: *Jagddivision 2* came from northern Germany, *Jagddivision 1* arrived from the Berlin area and *Jagddivision 7* came west from Bavaria to meet the raiding force.

It was an ideal night for the free-hunting tactics employed by the German crews, and during the hour that followed they rained retribution on those who were destroying their homeland. *Unteroffizier* Emil Nonenmacher of *III Gruppe* of *Nachtjagdgeschwader 2* based at Twenthe in Holland, piloting a Ju 88, joined the action shortly after the initial clash:

> As we climbed out of Twenthe we could see that a great battle was already in progress: there were aircraft burning in the air and on the ground; there was the occasional explosion in mid-air and much firing with tracer rounds. We kept on towards the scene of high activity for about five minutes, then suddenly we hit the

slipstream from one of the bombers. Now we were getting close to the bomber stream. It seemed that there was activity all around us—here an aircraft on fire, there someone firing, somewhere else an explosion on the ground. Yet it was a few more minutes before we actually caught sight of a bomber, its silhouette passing obliquely over my cockpit.

Now Nonenmacher was in the stream. It was a very clear night and he could see as many as fifteen bombers around him, all of them leaving condensation trails. He tried to move into a firing position behind the first aircraft he had seen, but he misjudged the approach and had to break away. It did not matter—there were plenty of others:

With so many targets visible I could take my pick, so I chose the nearest one in front of me—a Lancaster—and went after him. He was weaving gently. I set myself up for a deflection shot, aiming at a point one aircraft length ahead of the bomber. I opened fire and saw my rounds striking it. Then I paused, put my sight on the bomber again and fired another burst. After a few rounds my guns stopped firing—I had exhausted the ammunition in the drum magazines on my cannon.

Nonenmacher ordered his flight engineer to replace the ammunition drums, but in the meantime he had to let the bomber escape. As the crewman wrestled to fit new ammunition drums, Nonenmacher closed on another Lancaster:

I moved into a firing position about 100 metres astern and a little below it. By then the engineer had one of the cannon going so I pressed the firing button and saw my rounds striking the left wing. Soon afterwards both engines on that side burst into flames. He began to lose height and we could see the crew bailing out, it was so clear. The bomber took about six minutes to go down; when it reached the ground it blew up with a huge explosion.

MESSERSCHMITT BF 110G-4

Role: Three-seat night fighter.

Power: Two Daimler Benz DB 605B 12-cylinder, liquid-cooled, in-line engines each developing 1,475hp at take-off.

Armament: (Offensive) Various weapon mixes carried, but typically two Rheinmetall MK 108 30mm and two Mauser MG 151 20mm cannon mounted in the nose and two Oerlikon MG/FF 20mm cannon in a *Schräge Musik* installation firing obliquely upwards from the rear cabin; (defensive) two Rheinmetall MG 81 7.9mm machine guns on a hand-held installation in the cabin firing rearwards.

Performance: Maximum speed 342mph at 23,000ft; service ceiling 26,250ft.

Normal operational take-off weight: 20,700lb.

Dimensions: Span 53ft 4½in; length 42ft 9½in; wing area 413 sq ft.

Date of first production Bf 110G-4: June 1942.

Note: From the end of 1943, Bf 110Gs were fitted with *SN-2* AI radar as standard equipment and some machines also carried *Flensburg* homing receivers.

Several night fighters carried the recently introduced *Schräge Musik* installation, a pair of 20mm cannon in a fixed mounting firing obliquely forwards and upwards at an angle of 70 degrees. One pilot who used these weapons to effect was *Oberleutnant* Helmut Schulte, a Bf 110 pilot with *II Gruppe* of *NJG 5*, who later recalled:

> Normally our biggest problem was to find the bomber stream, but on this night we had no trouble. I found the enemy at a height of 6,000m [about 20,000ft]. I sighted a Lancaster and got underneath it and opened fire with [*Schräge Musik*]. Unfortunately [the guns] jammed so that only a few shots put out of action the starboard-inner motor. The bomber dived violently and turned to the north, but because of the good visibility we were able to keep him in sight. I now attempted a second attack after he had settled on his course, but because the Lancaster was now very slow, we always came out too far in front. I tried the *schräge Musik* again, and after another burst the bomber fell in flames.

The effectiveness of the attacks by Nonenmacher, Schulte and their comrades was fully evident to the crews of other bombers. Squadron Leader G. Graham, a Lancaster pilot with No 550 Squadron, recalled:

> We went in south of Cologne and were immediately met by the German fighters—I could say hundreds. It was a fantastic sight in the clear moonlight—aircraft going down in flames and exploding everywhere.

Flying Officer George Foley, flying as radar operator in one of the Lancaster Pathfinders, later recalled that he knew that things were beginning to go badly when he heard his pilot say, 'Better put your parachutes on, chaps—I've just seen the forty-second go down.' And the feelings of Lancaster pilot Flight Lieutenant Graham Ross were similar to those of many a bomber captain that night:

> I was very shaken at seeing so many aircraft going down in flames. I was scared by that, but still more scared at the thought that my own crew might be scared by it all.

The most successful German pilot during the action was *Oberleutnant* Martin Becker, flying a Bf 110G of *I Gruppe* of *NJG 6*, based at Mainz/Finthen. An experienced pilot, he already had nineteen victories to his credit. Becker had a well-honed technique for bringing down bombers, using his forward-firing cannon. He would approach his victim from slightly below and to one side, to avoid being seen by the rear gunner. When within about 100yds of the bomber, he would edge into position immediately behind and below it, then pull up his nose and rake the bomber with cannon shells as it passed across his gun sight. Becker used these tactics to great effect that night, shooting down a total of seven heavy bombers.

Because of the unusually large area covered by the raiding force, the *Luftwaffe* fighter controllers had great difficulty in determining its intended target. But if there were doubt as to where the raiders were going, there could be none about where they had been. The path of the raiding force running eastward from 'Ida' was clearly marked on the ground by a trail of wrecked and burning aircraft. Not until 1.08 a.m., two minutes before the first bombs were due to fall on Nuremberg, was the city mentioned in the radio broadcasts to night fighters.

As the badly mauled raiding force approached the target, the perfidious weather again took a hand in the proceedings. Instead of the predicted clear skies over the target, the bomber crews found a thick blanket of cloud. When the Pathfinder aircraft released their strings of target-markers, the latter vanished into the murk. The attack that followed was scattered and ineffective, with bombs falling over a wide area. A few bombs fell on the north-eastern part of the city, but the industrial quarter was virtually untouched. That the maximum-effort raid achieved so little illustrates, in the starkest terms, the vulnerability of an air-attack plan to the vagaries of the weather.

As the bombers began their return flights, many crews feared that the savage night fighter attacks would continue. Mercifully for them, this was not the case, however: as the bombers headed west, the night fighters lost contact and there were few engagements during the withdrawal.

Several of the aircraft heading for home bore the scars of earlier encounters with the enemy. One such was a Halifax of No 578 Squadron piloted by Pilot Officer Cyril Barton. On the way to the target the bomber had twice been attacked by night fighters. It had one engine knocked out, the intercom system was shot away, one of the fuel tanks was holed and the hydraulic supply to the three gun turrets had been cut, putting all three out of action. A misinterpreted signal from the pilot had been taken as an order to bail out, and the navigator, bomb-aimer and wireless operator had jumped from the aircraft.

Despite this catalogue of damage, Barton had continued doggedly to the target and dropped his bombs. Then he turned for home, using the North Star to calculate a rough heading. The Halifax made a landfall near Sunderland, well to the north of that intended, on the last of its fuel. Such determination to overcome all odds deserved success, but it was not to be. Shortly afterwards the fuel gave out and Barton had to attempt a crash-landing in the darkness. Suddenly a line of houses appeared in his path, and when he swerved to miss them the bomber stalled and struck the ground heavily, nose-first. The three crew members in the rear fuselage survived, but the gallant pilot was killed. For 'unsurpassed courage and devotion to duty', Cyril Barton later received the posthumous award of the Victoria Cross.

Other bombers limped home with all manner of damage. Flight Sergeant Ronald Reinelt of No 433 (Canadian) Squadron, for example, landed his Halifax at Manston with one engine knocked out and 32 square feet of the skinning of the starboard wing burned away.

Ninety-four of the 782 bombers that set out to attack Nuremberg failed to return. That loss rate, nearly 13 per cent, represented the greatest proportional loss rate ever suffered by so large a force during a single action. Forty-eight bombers returned with major battle damage, in some cases so serious that the aircraft had to be consigned to the scrap heap. As usual during such actions, the German night fighter losses were minimal—five aircraft destroyed and five damaged beyond repair.

Inevitably, an account of an air action leans towards descriptions of aircraft destroyed or damaged. To put the matter into proportion, however, it should be pointed out that of the 782 bombers that set out, more than 500 (over two-thirds) reached the target and returned without damage of any kind.

Following the Nuremberg disaster, there were dark rumours that the raiders had been betrayed—that the defenders had known the target beforehand and had arranged their dispositions accordingly. These rumours were repeated in some post-war accounts. The conspiracy theory finds no support in contemporary *Luftwaffe* records, however, nor in the later recollections of *Luftwaffe* personnel who took part in the action. If the defenders knew the location of the target beforehand, why did the night fighters gain most of their victories *along the route* to the target, and lose contact with the bombers after it? In truth, during the early months of 1944 the *Luftwaffe* night-fighter force was at the height of its prowess; and, on the night of 30/31 March 1944, almost everything had gone right for the defenders and several things had gone wrong for the raiders.

The *Luftwaffe* night-fighter force would never come close to repeating its success. In April 1944 RAF Bomber Command shifted the focus of its attack to targets in France and Belgium, as part of the softening-up operation preceding the Normandy invasion. These shallow-penetration attacks gave the night fighters little time to find the bomber stream and concentrate forces against it. When the night attacks on Germany resumed, after the invasion, the loss of territory in France allowed raiders attacking targets in the south of Germany to approach over friendly territory. Again, there was no opportunity to set up the sort of long-running fight that was so devastatingly successful during the final night in March 1944.

CHAPTER ELEVEN

Day of the Sturmgruppe

In the spring of 1944, the US daylight bombing offensive against Germany entered a new and more devastating phase. Now with continuous fighter escort all the way to and from their targets, the heavy bombers were tearing the heart out of German industry. The Americans were on the point of establishing air superiority over the German homeland, and for the time being it seemed that the Luftwaffe could do little about it. The long-term answer to the problem was the Messerschmitt Me 262 jet fighter, which alone had the speed to avoid the American escort fighters and the firepower to destroy the heavy bombers; its service career will be described in the next chapter. As a stop-gap until the revolutionary new fighter became available in quantity, the Luftwaffe formed a special type of bomber-destroyer unit manned by intrepid volunteer pilots—the Sturmgruppe.

BY THE BEGINNING of 1944 the *Luftwaffe* had pulled back virtually all of its day fighter units from the battle fronts and redeployed them to protect the homeland. But still it was not enough. During actions against the US raiding formations, the defending fighter units regularly found themselves outnumbered over their own territory by the hoards of wide-ranging escort fighters. Moreover, the P-51B Mustang, in service in large numbers, had a performance superior to that of any of its opponents, and the type was inflicting heavy losses. By the end of April, the defenders' situation had deteriorated to the point that *Generalmajor* Adolf Galland, the *Luftwaffe*'s Inspector of Fighters, was moved to report to his superiors:

> Between January and April 1944 our day fighter arm lost more than 1,000 pilots. They included our best *Staffel*, *Gruppe* and *Geschwader* commanders . . . The time has come when our force is within sight of collapse.

Even more serious than these losses was the fact that the defending fighter units were not shooting down enough enemy bombers to blunt the American attacks. The situation was completely different from that during the Regensburg raid in August 1943, when *Jagdgruppe 50* had only bombers to contend with and delivered repeated set-piece attacks until its aircraft exhausted their ammunition. Now, if the defending fighters did get through to the bombers, there was usually time for only one or at most two brief firing passes before the escorts arrived in force.

The *Luftwaffe* found itself enmeshed in a vicious 'Catch-22' situation. Its specialized bomber-destroyer types, the twin-engine Messerschmitt Bf 110s and Me 410s, carried hefty batteries of cannon and rockets that were highly effective against the American bombers. But these planes were relatively slow and un-

---

FOCKE WULF FW 190A-8

(Details for Sturmbock *version in parentheses)*

Role: Single-seat, general-purpose day fighter (single-seat bomber-destroyer).
Power: One BMW 801D-2 14-cylinder, air-cooled, radial engine developing 1,770hp at take-off.
Armament: Four MG 151 20mm cannon in the wings; two MG 131 13mm machine guns above the engine. (Two Rheinmetall Borsig MK 108 30mm cannon in place of the two MG 151 20mm cannon mounted mid-way along the wings.)
Performance: Maximum speed 402mph at 18,000ft (about 35mph slower); climb to 19,650ft, 9min 54sec (climbing performance considerably worse).
Normal operational take-off weight: 9,660lb (10,060lb).
Dimensions: Span 34ft 5½in; length 29ft 4½in; wing area 197 sq ft.
Date of first production FW 190A-8: January 1944.

---

wieldy and they often suffered heavy losses at the hands of the escorts. The less heavily armed Bf 109 and FW 190 single-engine fighters had the speed to avoid the escorts and get through to the bombers, but they lacked the firepower to enable pilots of average ability to knock down bombers during the necessarily short firing passes.

In the 'try anything' mood prevalent in the *Luftwaffe*, a new operational concept emerged to counter the enemy bomber formations. The idea centred on the use of a *Gruppe* of about thirty heavily armed FW 190s, fitted with extra armour and flown by volunteer pilots, that would move in *en masse* behind an enemy bomber formation to engage it from close range. This was the *Sturmgruppe*. The heavyweight FW 190s would be no match for the American escorts in combat, so the *Sturmgruppe* was itself to be escorted into action by two *Gruppen* of lightly armed Bf 109s; the latter were fitted with uprated engines and their task was to hold off the American fighters long enough for the Focke Wulfs to deliver their blow.

A new version of the FW 190, nicknamed the '*Sturmbock*' (battering ram), was produced specially for use with the new tactics. This carried two MK 108 30mm cannon in the wings, powerful weapons with a rate of fire of 600 rounds a minute. On average, three hits with the 18oz high-explosive/incendiary rounds were sufficient to send a heavy bomber falling out of control. The *Sturmbock* could carry only 55 rounds per gun, enough for just over five seconds' firing. Because the weapon had a relatively low muzzle velocity and was ineffective at long range, the new tactics called for the German pilots to close to within 100yds of a heavy bomber before they opened fire.

As they moved in on their targets, the *Sturmbock* pilots would have to brave the defensive crossfire from the bombers. To give them a reasonable chance of survival, the modified FW 190 carried twice the weight of armour of the standard fighter version. The heavier armament and armour added about 400lb to the aircraft and imposed corresponding reductions in manoeuvrability, maximum speed and climbing performance.

The *Sturmgruppen* were to be élite units. Before a volunteer was accepted, he had to sign a document stating that he was prepared to press home his attacks on enemy bombers to short range and that if the guns failed to destroy the enemy plane he would ram it. Any pilot who signed the affidavit and then failed to carry out its conditions was liable to be court-martialled on a charge of cowardice in the face of the enemy, and those found guilty would face a firing squad. Nobody was forced to sign the affidavit, however, and those who did not wish to do so were not accepted into the *Sturmgruppen*.

By this stage of the war, the American bomber columns were sometimes as much as a hundred miles long. Usually there was a large force of escorts at the head of the force, with small units sweeping the flanks. The German plan was to vector the *Sturmgruppe* into the bomber stream mid-way along its length, where the escort would be at its weakest.

Under the previous tactics, German fighter pilots flew in pairs or in fours to attack the enemy bombers, usually from head-on, and individual pilots decided when to open fire and when to break away. The *Sturmgruppe* pilots were to do things differently, and their tactics were more rigid than any used hitherto. The FW 190s were to fly in nine-aircraft *Staffeln*, with the leader in the middle and the aircraft on each side flying a few yards apart in echelon. Succeeding *Staffeln* would follow close behind that of the leader. The *Sturmgruppe* leader was to manoeuvre his force behind a formation of enemy bombers, then allocate his *Staffeln* to attack different parts of it. Each *Staffel* was to continue firing at the bombers for as long as there was ammunition for the heavy cannon, then the aircraft were to turn away together.

The essence of the *Sturmgruppe* tactics was a short but extremely sharp attack, delivered *en masse* against a single combat box formation of enemy bombers. Then the Focke Wulfs and their covering Messerschmitts were to leave the scene in high-speed dives, hoping to get well clear before the hoard of vengeful Mustangs and Thunderbolts arrived in the area.

Thus the *Sturmgruppe* differed from other *Luftwaffe* fighter units in three fundamental respects: in the type of aircraft it flew, in the tactics it employed and in the calibre of the men that served in it. The first such unit to be formed, *IV Gruppe* of *Jagdgeschwader 3*, received its complement of aircraft and pilots in May 1944 and began training for the new role immediately. Two other *Jagdgeschwader*, *JG 4* and *JG 300*, were each to convert one *Gruppe* to the new role as and when sufficient *Sturmbock* aircraft became available.

The first full-scale use of the new tactics was on 7 July 1944, against part of a force of 1,129 Flying Fortresses and Liberators attacking industrial targets in the Leipzig area. Fighter ace *Major* Walther Dahl led the attack formation, which comprised the *Sturmgruppe* with two *Gruppen* of Bf 109s providing top cover—about ninety aircraft assembled into one huge formation. The *Luftwaffe* fighter controller guided Dahl into visual contact with a column of bombers, and the latter led his force into the stream behind a formation of Liberators belonging to the 14th Combat Wing. There were no escorts in the area, and, as the *Sturmgruppe* closed in, the *Staffeln* moved into arrow-head formation, preparing to attack. The pilot of each Focke Wulf selected a Liberator and advanced unswervingly towards it. The American gunners put up a vigorous and spectacular return fire, making the sky alive with sparkling tracer rounds. Obeying the strict order to withhold their fire until the *Staffel* leader opened up, the German pilots could only grit our teeth and continue moving forwards. *Leutnant* Walther Hagenah, one of the pilots belonging to *JG 3*'s *Sturmgruppe*, described the mood as he closed in on the enemy bombers:

> It was essential that we held our fire until we were right up close against the bombers. We were to advance like Frederick the Great's infantrymen, holding our fire until we could see 'the whites of the enemies' eyes'.

In fact, the extra armour gave the Focke Wulf pilots considerable protection, and few of the attacks were knocked down by the return fire. The *Sturmböcke* slid into firing positions about 100yds behind the enemy bombers and opened a withering barrage. From that range the German pilots could hardly miss, and, as the 3cm explosive rounds struck home, the B-24 formation dissolved in front of them.

That day, the US 2nd Bomb Division lost 28 Liberators, most of them during the *Sturmgruppe* action. The unit hardest hit was the 492nd Bomb Group, which lost a dozen planes in rapid succession. Walther Hagenah was credited with the destruction of one B-24. The *Sturmgruppe* lost nine fighters shot down, and three more crash-landed; five of its pilots were killed. By the standards of the day, it had been a highly successful defensive operation for the *Luftwaffe*. Walther Hagenah was in action with his *Sturmgruppe* on 18 and 20 July, when he destroyed a B-17 on each occasion, and on 3 August, when he shot down a B-24.

Although the pilots had signed affidavits indicating a willingness to ram enemy bombers if other means of destroying them failed, only rarely was it necessary to adopt this course. Once a Focke Wulf reached a firing position, it could usually achieve a kill with its heavy cannon. Of the pilots who did carry out ramming attacks, about half escaped without serious injury. One who did not was *Obergefreiter* Heinz Papenburg of *JG 4*'s *Sturmgruppe*, whose cannon failed at

---

CONSOLIDATED B-24J LIBERATOR

Role: Ten-seat, four-engine heavy bomber.

Power: Four Pratt & Whitney R-1830 Twin Wasp 14-cylinder, air-cooled, radial engines each developing 1,200hp at take-off.

Armament: (Offensive) The bomb load depended on the radius of action required but was typically 6,000lb; (defensive) ten Browning .5in machine guns, two each in powered turrets in the nose, in the tail and above and below the fuselage and one each in the waist positions.

Performance: Formation cruising speed (with full bomb load) 185mph at 22,000ft; tactical radius of action (flying in formation, with operational fuel reserves and with 6,000lb of bombs) 600 miles.

Normal operational take-off weight: 56,000lb.

Dimensions: Span 110ft; length 67ft 2in; wing area 1,048 sq ft.

Date of first production B-24J: Late 1943.

the vital moment during an attack on 27 August. He continued on and destroyed a B-24 by ramming. One wing of the Focke Wulf was torn away during the collision, and as the pilot jumped from the spinning fighter he struck the tail and broke both legs. The unfortunate pilot descended by parachute and had to take the shock of the landing on his shattered limbs.

The American countermeasure to the *Sturmgruppe* tactics was to send large-scale fighter sweeps in front of the bombers and along their flanks, with the aim of breaking up the ponderous German attack formations before the could reach the bombers. Once it had been scattered, there was no way in which an attack formation could reassemble if enemy fighters were about, and the operation had then to be abandoned. Usually, the American countermeasures were successful, though from time to time a *Sturmgruppe* did succeed in getting through to the bombers to deliver an attack. On 2 November 1944 two of these units mounted separate and successful attacks on American heavy-bomber formations. Thirty-nine aircraft of *JG 3* attacked the 91st Bomb Group and knocked down thirteen Flying Fortresses, including two by ramming. Later that day, 22 *Sturmbock* fighters of *JG 4* attacked the 457th Bomb Group. Sergeant Bernard Sitek witnessed the latter engagement from the ball turret of his B-17:

> Everything happened pretty fast, as it usually does when the Germans offer any opposition. We had been off the bomb run about ten minutes when vapour trails from fighters started to fill the sky. Friendly or enemy, was the question on everybody's mind. We soon learned the answer. They were FW 190s and Me 109s forming up for one of those wolfpack attacks. At first it appeared that they were on the same level as our Box, the High Box, but as they came closer they lowered themselves for an attack on the Low and the Lead Boxes.

In the action that followed, the Low and the Lead Boxes of the formation lost nine bombers within just over a minute. In both cases the American escort fighters arrived too late to prevent the attacks, but they were able to exact a heavy price from the *Sturmgruppen* involved. Of the 61 *Sturmbock* aircraft taking part in the actions, 31 were shot down; seventeen German pilots were killed and seven were wounded.

In the weeks that followed, a shortage of fuel—the result of repeated air attacks on German oil refineries—limited the ability of the *Luftwaffe* to retaliate effectively. Successful *Sturmgruppe* actions became fewer and increasingly far between. The last one of note took place on 14 January 1945, when aircraft of *JG 300* delivered a sharp attack on B-17s of the 390th Bomb Group and shot down all eight aircraft in one squadron's formation. During the action five *Sturmgruppe* pilots were killed and two were wounded.

Although the *Sturmgruppen* achieved the occasional spectacular success against individual bomber formations during the autumn and winter of 1944, after an impressive beginning their operations became increasingly difficult and costly. It was not that the tactics were at fault or that the pilots lacked the determination necessary to carry them out: it was simply that no tactical method was likely often to succeed in the face of such overwhelming enemy air superiority.

CHAPTER TWELVE

The Jets get their Chance

*By mid-1944, the development of the piston-engine fighter aircraft had reached a
dead end. Then, on cue, the jet-propelled fighter appeared on the scene, offering a
huge advance in performance. Faced by numerically superior foes on all fronts
and with the Fatherland under sustained and devastating air attack, the Luftwaffe channelled enormous resources into bringing the Messerschmitt Me 262 jet
aircraft into mass production. Here, it seemed, lay the technical innovation that
would re-establish air superiority over Germany and beyond its frontiers. For
their part, the Allies had soon become aware of the existence of the new aircraft
and dreaded the time when it would be introduced into combat. In the event, both
sides underestimated the difficulty of getting the turbojet engine to function relia-
bly, and the difficulty of mass-producing it.*

BY THE FINAL YEAR of the Second World War, the performance of the
piston-engine fighter was close to its physical limit. The problem was fundamental to this form of power unit and there was no way to circumvent it. The
rotational power of the piston engine was converted into forward thrust by the
propeller, but, as speeds approached 500mph, the efficiency of the propeller decreased rapidly, and a huge increase in engine power was necessary to give a
small increase in maximum speed.

A few figures will serve to illustrate the point. In round terms, the Merlin engine powering the Spitfire Mk I developed 1,000hp, which gave the fighter a
maximum speed of about 300mph at sea level. At that speed, the propeller was
about 80 per cent efficient and the 1,000lb of thrust it produced equalled the drag
from the Spitfire's airframe. Now consider the amount of engine power needed to
propel that same Spitfire at twice that speed, 600mph. Drag rises with the square
of speed, so doubling the speed meant quadrupling the drag. Thus 1,000lb of drag
at 300mph became 4,000lb of drag at 600mph, and to overcome that the aircraft
needed 4,000lb of thrust. It can be shown that this was the equivalent of 6,400hp.
At 600mph the efficiency of the propeller was only about 53 per cent, however.
So to drive the aircraft at that speed the engine needed to develop not 6,400hp but
12,000. In 1945 the best piston engines for fighters produced just over one horse-
power for each pound of weight, so a piston engine able to propel the fighter at
600mph would have weighed some 11,000lb—about double the all-up weight of
an early production Spitfire.

For flight at high speeds, the turbojet was a fundamentally more efficient form
of powerplant. It produced its thrust directly, and that thrust remained nearly constant throughout the aircraft's speed range. The two Jumo turbojets fitted to the
Me 262 delivered a total of 3,960lb of thrust for a total weight of only 2,650lb and

gave the fighter a maximum level speed of 540mph. No piston engine then in existence or under consideration offered a comparable thrust-to-weight ratio.

So much for the technical rationale for the jet fighter. The business of getting Me 262 into service in the *Luftwaffe* would involve a lengthy and tortuous military-political process. Yet, despite its superb performance, the aircraft would fail utterly to live up to its promise. Some commentators have attributed this to ineptitude on the part of Adolf Hitler for insisting it be used initially as a fighter-bomber. Others have said that the *Luftwaffe* failed to push the development and production of the aircraft with sufficient vigour. It has even been suggested that, had the Me 262 been brought into service more rapidly, the war might have taken a different course. In this chapter we shall examine the facts and the myths concerning this fascinating combat aircraft.

* * *

The Me 262 made its first successful flight on jet power in July 1942 and it was soon achieving speeds in excess of 430mph in level flight; as more powerful versions of the Jumo 004 engine became available, its maximum speed rose above the 500mph mark. So long as the power units worked properly, the aircraft had a sparkling performance, but the early turbojets had a poor record of reliability. Flame-outs and turbine failures occurred with disconcerting regularity, and the prototypes spent much of their time on the ground undergoing engine changes.

The turbojet ran at much higher temperatures, and at far greater rotational speeds, than the piston engine. As a result, those who designed the early jet engines had to overcome a host of fundamentally new problems, and in many cases did so from first principles. One of the most intractable problems facing the German engineers was a lack of nickel and chromium. These essential ingredients for the manufacture of high-temperature-resistant steel alloys were in critically short supply in wartime Germany, and neither was available for the jet engine programme. As a result, Junkers technicians had to demonstrate considerable ingenuity in devising substitute materials for the Jumo 004 engine. The combustion chambers, for example, were made from ordinary steel with a spray-coating of aluminium to increase their ability to withstand high temperatures. Such measures were only partially successful, however, and the running life of the early 004s rarely exceeded ten hours before an engine change became necessary.

From the summer of 1943, the *Luftwaffe* was under severe pressure to get the Me 262 into mass production. Although the Jumo 004 was insufficiently reliable to allow the design to be frozen for such, the *Luftwaffe*, anticipating that any problems would soon be solved, ordered the Messerschmitt company to begin tooling up for the mass production of airframes (some of the first jigs were destroyed during the attack on Regensburg, described in Chapter 8). In the months that followed, the need to get the jet fighter into service became steadily greater.

As described in the previous chapter, the fighter units defending Germany were suffering heavy losses and were able to destroy only a small proportion of the attacking bombers. The available day fighter types had either the firepower to

---

MESSERSCHMITT ME 262A

Role: Single-seat jet fighter or fighter-bomber.
Power: Two Junkers Juno 004A jet engines each developing 1,980lb of thrust.
Armament: (Fighter role) Four MK 108 30mm cannon; (fighter-bomber role) two 30mm cannon and two 550lb bombs carried externally under the fuselage.
Performance: Maximum speed 540mph at 19,500ft; climb to 19,680ft, 6min 48sec.
Normal operational take-off weight: 14,100lb.
Dimensions: Span 40ft 11½in; length 34ft 9½in; wing area 234 sq ft.
Date of first production Me 262A: Spring 1944.

---

destroy the heavy bombers or the performance to engage the American escort fighters, but none of them had both. The Me 262 promised to solve this problem at a stroke: it was faster than any Allied fighter, and its armament of four MK 108 30mm cannon was sufficiently powerful to tear apart the structures of heavy bombers.

In the spring of 1944, a test unit was formed at Lechfeld in Bavaria to introduce the Me 262 into service and train a cadre of pilots to fly it. Yet, although the reliability of the Jumo 004 had improved slightly by then, the engine still required skilful handling. Throttle movements had to be made slowly, otherwise there was a risk of the engine overheating or suffering a flame-out. Once he had throttled back and reduced speed on the landing approach, a pilot was committed to landing. If thereafter he advanced the throttles to go round again, the 004's poor acceleration meant that the aircraft was likely to hit the ground before it gained sufficient speed to climb away. Clearly, the aircraft was not yet ready for combat, nor was it a suitable vehicle for fighter pilots of average or below-average ability.

Meanwhile, pressure was being exerted on the Me 262 programme from a quite different source. The most potent threat then facing Adolf Hitler was the expected Anglo-American invasion of north-west Europe. If it succeeded, his forces would have to fight a two-front war against enemies with numerically superior forces. The critical time for such an invasion would be in the hours immediately following the initial landings, as the troops sought to establish defensive positions ashore before German ground forces could mount their counter-attack. If the Allied troops could be subjected to repeated bombing and strafing attacks as they came ashore, they might still be in disarray when the German *Panzer* divisions arrived on the scene. And if that happened, it might be possible to defeat the landing operation with heavy losses.

Given the scale of the Allied fighter cover to be expected over the beach-head, Hitler believed, correctly, that only the Me 262 was fast enough to get through to the landing area and attack with any certainty of success. During discussions, the *Führer* was assured that, if required, the Me 262 could carry a couple of two 550lb bombs, and from then on the aircraft featured prominently in his anti-invasion plans. There can be little doubt that the Me 262 could have performed the task, and that if a landing operation ran into difficulties—as would happen at Omaha Beach on D-Day—such harassment could be decisive. If there were only a few jet aircraft available, they could be used to much greater effect in attacking the troops coming ashore than in battling with the hoards of Allied aircraft in the skies above the landings. *Generalfeldmarschall* Erhard Milch, the *Luftwaffe* officer responsible for aircraft production, acknowledged the importance of the Me 262 as a fighter-bomber. But he continued to devote his efforts to getting it into service with the fighter force as quickly as possible. So far as he was concerned, the fighter-bomber version could come later.

Matters came to a head on 23 May 1944 when Göring, Milch and other senior *Luftwaffe* officers were summoned to a conference on aircraft production at Hitler's headquarters at Berchtesgaden. When the Me 262 was mentioned, the *Führer* asked, 'I thought the 262 was coming as a high-speed bomber? How many of the 262s already manufactured can carry bombs?' Milch replied that to date none had been modified for this purpose: the aircraft was being manufactured exclusively as a fighter. There was an awkward silence, then Milch dug himself further into the pit when he stated that the new aircraft would not be able to carry bombs unless there were extensive design changes. Hearing that, Hitler lost his composure and excitedly interrupted his *Generalfeldmarschall*: 'Never mind! I wanted only one 250-kilo [550lb] bomb.'

As the *Führer* realized the implications of what he had been told, he became increasingly angry. After the assurances he had been given on the ease with which the Me 262 could be modified to carry bombs, no preparatory work had been done to enable it to do so. The Allied invasion might begin at any moment, and it seemed that the weapon on which he had pinned high hopes had been snatched from his hands. Hitler delivered a savage denunciation of the duplicity of the *Luftwaffe* officers present and said that he would hold Göring personally responsible for ensuring that the Me 262 was introduced into service in the fighter-bomber role as rapidly as possible.

It must be stressed, however, that, at the time Hitler delivered his now-famous edict that every Me 262 possible be modified for use as a fighter-bomber, the continuing unreliability of its 004 engine precluded the aircraft's operational use *in any role*. Nothing had changed two weeks later when, on 6 June, the Allied troops stormed ashore in Normandy. By the end of that morning the invaders were firmly established ashore, and the opportunity for Me 262s to achieve a decisive impact on the landings had passed.

The formation of the first Me 262 jet fighter-bomber unit was pushed ahead with all speed, and near the end of June the 3rd *Staffel* of *Kampfgeschwader 51* began to re-equip with these aircraft. On 20 July the jet fighter-bomber unit was declared operational and moved to Chateaudun near Paris, with nine aircraft each equipped to carry two 550lb bombs. To reduce losses, and to minimize the risk of one of the new planes falling into enemy hands, pilots had orders not to descend below 4,000m (13,000ft) over hostile territory. The bombs were released in shallow dives from above that altitude, an inaccurate type of attack which meant that the jet fighter-bombers achieved little against small targets such as bridges or vehicles. Moreover, the short running life of the 004 restricted flying and kept most of the aircraft on the ground.

Also at this time, the fighter ace *Major* Walter Nowotny took command of the Me 262 test unit at Lechfeld and the latter was re-named *Kommando 'Nowotny'*. The unit possessed fifteen early-production machines unsuitable for modification for the fighter-bomber role. The serviceability of these aircraft was poor, and only rarely would it have more than four of the jet fighters available to fly. *Kommando 'Nowotny'* carried out test interceptions using single Me 262s against Allied reconnaissance aircraft, and in the course of August the jet fighter achieved its first kills—two Mosquitos, a Spitfire, a Lightning and a B-17.

In September 1944, following a series of incremental improvements, the running life of the turbojet at last reached the 25-hour mark. That was not a lot by normal standards, but it was sufficient to allow the design to be frozen so that mass production could begin. During that month Hitler rescinded his edict that all Me 262s coming off the production lines be issued only to fighter-bomber units. By then there were more than a hundred Me 262 fighter airframes standing idle awaiting engines, and as the latter became available in quantity these aircraft were completed. During September 91 Me 262 fighters and fighter-bombers were delivered to the *Luftwaffe*—more than in the previous two months put together.

Following the change of policy, *Kommando 'Nowotny'* re-equipped with new-built fighters and had a strength of 23 aircraft at the end of September. The unit was declared ready for operations and moved to Achmer and Hesepe in north-west Germany to operate in the interceptor role. Several accounts on the Me 262 have stated that the *Führer*'s edict was responsible for keeping the aircraft out of the hands of German fighter pilots until late in the war. The available documentary evidence makes it clear that this was not the case, however. In fact, Hitler's decree delayed the introduction into combat by the first Me 262 fighter *Gruppe*, with aircraft fitted with production engines, by less than *three weeks*.

In the event, the operational deployment of *Kommando 'Nowotny'* was a complete failure, and the *Führer*'s edict had nothing to do with that. Although the Jumo 004 now gave a slightly longer running life than before, its serviceability remained poor. Furthermore, as with any new type, the airframe of the Me 262 had its share of 'bugs' to be ironed out. One of the most serious problems resulted from the use of low-quality tyres made from synthetic and reclaimed rubber: a heavy landing at the jet fighter's touch-down speed of around 120mph often caused a blow-out, which sometimes led to damage to the undercarriage.

The Allies quickly discovered the Achilles' heel of the jet fighter—its vulnerability to attack while flying at low speed immediately after take-off or on the landing approach. Fighters regularly patrolled over the airfields used by jet fighters, causing almost continual harassment. Moreover, away from the airfields, the horizontal speed advantage of the Me 262 over Allied fighter types was often negated when the latter attacked from above in high-speed dives. These points were illustrated on 7 October when *Kommando 'Nowotny'* scrambled five Me 262s—the largest number of jet fighters yet sent into combat—against formations of American bombers heading for targets in central Germany. Passing over Achmer at 15,000ft, Lieutenant Urban Drew, in a Mustang of the 361st Fighter Group, noticed a pair of jet fighters commence their take-off runs. He waited until the enemy planes were airborne, then rolled into a high-speed dive, followed by his wingman. Drew rapidly caught up with the Me 262s and shot down both before they reached fighting speed. Later that day a third jet fighter was lost during a separate action with escort fighters. Thus the first multi-aircraft action by *Kommando 'Nowotny'* cost the unit three Me 262s destroyed and one pilot killed, in return for three American bombers shot down. In the course of its first full month of operations on the Western Front, *Kommando 'Nowotny'* claimed the destruction of four American heavy bombers, twelve fighters and three reconnaissance aircraft. In achieving this, however, the unit lost six Me 262s in combat and a further seven destroyed and nine damaged in accidents or following technical failures. It was not an auspicious start to the jet fighter's combat career.

Then, on 8 November, the *Kommando* suffered the most grievous blow of all. After getting caught up in a low-level dogfight with Mustangs, Walter Nowotny was shot down and killed. *Generalmajor* Galland happened to be at the Achmer that day, on a visit of inspection to determine why the Me 262 unit had failed to achieve more. Galland saw enough to realize that Nowotny had been given an impossible task. The latter had to introduce a completely new type of fighter into operational service, though many of his pilots had received no proper conversion training. Serviceability was poor, and rarely could the unit fly more than half a dozen sorties per day. As a result, the Allied air forces, which had massive numerical superiority in the area, usually dictated the terms on which the jets had to fight. Galland ordered the Me 262 unit to return to Lechfeld for further training and in order that the aircraft could be modified to overcome some of their defects. He realized that it had been a mistake to commit the jet fighters into combat in such small numbers. If the new fighter were to have a decisive effect, a much larger force would need to be assembled. The formation of the first full *Geschwader* of Me 262 fighters, *JG 7*, had begun, but it would be some time before the unit was fully operational.

Meanwhile, what of the Me 262 as a fighter-bomber? By the latter part of 1944 these aircraft equipped two full *Gruppen*, *I* and *II* of *Kampfgeschwader 51*. Single aircraft delivered attacks on Allied airfields and troop positions in France, Holland and Belgium. Again, due to the small number of aircraft involved and the small tonnage of bombs they carried, these attacks achieved little.

By the beginning of 1945, new Me 262s were coming off the assembly lines at an encouraging rate. Production was running at 36 aircraft a week, and so far about 600 had been delivered to the *Luftwaffe*. Yet the Quartermaster General's records for 10 January 1945 show that only about 60 Me 262s (only 10 per cent of those manufactured so far) were serving with operational units, and none with operational day fighter units, 52 served with *Kampfgeschwader 51* operating in the fighter-bomber role, four were operating as night fighters and five were employed in the short-range reconnaissance role—this some four months after Hitler had rescinded his edict that the Me 262 be employed only in the fighter-bomber role. What had gone wrong?

Although a number of Me 262 fighter *Gruppen* were preparing to go into action, this preliminary work was taking much longer than expected. *III Gruppe of*

Jagdgeschwader 7 had its full complement of aircraft and was working up at airfields in the Berlin area; *I Gruppe* was forming at Kaltenkirchen near Hamburg, as was *II Gruppe* at Brandenburg/Briest. Also at this time, *Kampfgeschwader 54*, a bomber unit, was converting to the Me 262 and its pilots were training to operate the aircraft in the *fighter* role. The unit was redesignated *KG (Jäger) 54*, and this diversion of Me 262s from 'pure' fighter units has been linked to Hitler's earlier insistence that initially the type be used as a fighter-bomber. But by early 1945 the issues were quite different. Pilots assigned to *Luftwaffe* day fighter units did not receive training in instrument flying, as a move to shorten the training time and save resources. Pilots assigned to bomber, reconnaissance and night-fighter units received training in instrument flying as a matter of course, and *KG(J) 54* was to operate in the bad-weather interception role.

As we have seen, early in January 1945 there were about 60 Me 262s operational with fighter-bomber, night-fighter and reconnaissance units. A further 150 of these aircraft were flying with day fighter units, working up for action or providing pilot conversion training. About 30 Me 262s were serving with the various test centres, and about 150 Me 262s had been destroyed by enemy action in the air or on the ground, or in flying accidents. That accounted for about 400 Me 262s. What had happened to the remaining 200 of these aircraft, about one-third of those built? Many were tied up in the German rail system. After their acceptance test-flights, most of the Me 262s were dismantled and transported to the operational units by rail, in order to save precious aviation fuel. With the German rail network now under systematic attack from Allied strategic bombers, many of the crated jet fighters were destroyed in transit or were stranded in sidings from which they never emerged. Moreover, the attacks on the rail system made it difficult to move fuel and spare parts—including the all-important replacement engines—to the operational airfields.

Adding to the problems of the jet fighter units, their airfields were repeatedly bombed and for much of the time they were patrolled by Allied fighters. This, combined with the poor weather over Germany during the winter of 1944–45, frequently brought jet-flying training to a halt. Even without such impediments, it is difficult enough to introduce a new combat aircraft type into large-scale service. Considering the daunting array of difficulties, it is hardly surprising that the formation of a large and effective jet-fighter force suffered continual slippage.

The Me 262s returned to the day battle on 9 February 1945, when *I Gruppe* of *KG(J) 54* put up about ten aircraft to counter a multi-pronged attack by American heavy bombers against targets in central Germany. The German ex-bomber pilots had received only a sketchy training in air-to-air combat, however, and this was neither the time nor the place to learn its finer points. The escorting Mustangs shot down six Me 262s, while the jet fighters were able to inflict damage on only one B-17. Bomber ace *Oberstleutnant* Volprecht von Riedesel, the *Geschwader* commander, was one of the German pilots killed that day.

Two weeks later, on the 25th, *KG(J) 54* had another bad day when its *II Gruppe* lost no fewer than twelve Me 262s, six in air combat, four during a strafing attack on its airfield and two more in flying accidents. *Major* Hansgeorg

Bätcher, a highly experienced bomber pilot, was appointed to command the *Geschwader*. In Bätcher's view, the unit had been sent into operations prematurely, and his first act was to withdraw it from action for further training. Despite the difficulties experienced by the ex-bomber pilots, he felt that, in the circumstances, the decision to use pilots with blind-flying training to fly the Me 262 in the fighter role was correct. It was winter, and on several days the bad weather prevented other jet fighter units from operating.

It was mid-February before *III Gruppe* of *Jagdgeschwader 7* was ready to go into action. On 21 February a force of Mustangs of the 479th Fighter Group, on patrol in the Berlin area, encountered about fifteen Me 262s—by far the largest number yet seen. And, as the American formation leader reported, for the first time these aircraft were handled in an aggressive manner:

> Bounce was directed at Red Flight, as Squadron was making a shallow turn to the left from an easterly direction. Bounce came from 3 o'clock position at our level by four Me 262s flying the usual American combat formation, looking like P-51s with drop tanks. Our Red Flight broke into jets but they crossed in front of our flight up and away. A second flight of four Me 262s flying in American combat formation then made a bounce from the rear, 6 o'clock high. Our flight turned into this second Me 262 flight and the Me 262s broke, climbing up and away. At this time the first flight of Me 262s came back on us again from above and to the rear. We broke into this flight and this kept up for three or four breaks, neither ourselves or Jerry being able to get set or close in for a shot. Each time we would break they would climb straight ahead, outdistancing us. Within the Jerry flight the Number 4 man, while turning, would fall behind and slightly above, so that it was necessary to take on this Number 4 man or he would slice in on our tail if our Flight would take on the rest of the Jerry flight.

The report exemplified the sort of inconclusive action that resulted when well-handled jets confronted well-handled Mustangs. Unless it had the advantage of surprise, the Me 262 was no real threat to the latter.

During the course of February, *Leutnant* Rudolf Rademacher of *III./JG 7* showed what a well-handled Me 262 could achieve. After shooting down a Spitfire reconnaissance aircraft near Brunswick on 1 February, he was credited the

---

NORTH AMERICAN P-51D MUSTANG

Role: Single-seat, long-range escort fighter and fighter-bomber.

Power: One Rolls-Royce/Packard Merlin V-1650-7 12-cylinder, liquid-cooled, in-line engine developing 1,450hp at take-off.

Armament: Four or six Browning .5in machine guns in the wings; provision for two 1,000lb bombs or ten 5in rockets under the wings.

Performance: (Clean) Maximum speed 437mph at 25,000ft; initial rate of climb 3,475ft/min; operational radius of action (with two 110-gallon drop tanks) 900 miles.

Dimensions: Span 37ft; length 32ft 3in; wing area 233 sq ft.

Date of first production P-51D: Summer 1944.

destruction of six heavy bombers and a Mustang, to bring his score during that month to eight victories.

Only in March 1945 did Me 262s launch large-scale attacks on American bomber formations. On the 3rd there were 29 Me 262 sorties, mainly by *III./JG 7*, in response to the US attacks on Magdeburg, Brunswick, Hanover, Chemnitz and other targets. The jet-fighter units claimed the destruction of six bombers and two fighters, in return for one Me 262 lost. American records list nine bombers and eight fighters lost on that day, and mention no Me 262 destroyed.

The Me 262 fighter units saw little action during the next two weeks, and their next great exertion was on 18 March. On that day 37 of the jets took off to engage a large force of American bombers making for Berlin. Twenty-eight jet-fighter pilots reported making contact with the enemy and claimed the destruction of twelve bombers and one fighter (all except two of the bombers were claimed by *JG 7*); from American records, it appears likely that only eight heavy bombers fell to the Me 262s. Two jet fighters were lost during the action. During each of the following seven days there were pitched battles between Me 262s and American formations, with a similar ratio of losses between the two sides.

On the 30th the *Luftwaffe* put up 31 jet fighters to engage US bomber forces attacking Hamburg, Bremen and Wilhelmshaven. The jet fighters were at their most vulnerable when taking off or landing, and Mustang pilot Captain Robert Sargent, of the 330th Fighter Group, exploited this weakness to the full:

I saw two enemy aircraft taking off from Kaltenkirchen airfield. I called them in and we split-essed down on them. Unfortunately due to their camouflage we lost them for a second and when we got down to their level I was able to pick up just one of them. From here on it was easy. My air speed was 430mph and I estimated his as being about 230mph. As we closed I gave him a long burst and noticed strikes immediately, the left unit began to pour white smoke and large pieces of the canopy came off. The pilot baled out. We were at 300 feet at this time and the plane dove into the ground and exploded, causing a large oil-like fire which went out almost at once. The pilot's chute did not open fully and the last I saw of him was on the ground near the plane with the chute streaming out behind him. Lt Kunz did a splendid job of covering my tail and after the encounter we pulled up and looked for the second jet. But when we sighted him he was going balls-out for central Germany and we couldn't overtake him.

The Me 262 pilot involved, *Leutnant* Erich Schulte of *I./JG 7*, was killed. In the course of the fighting that day, the jet fighters claimed the destruction of three enemy bombers and three fighters, for the loss of three of their own aircraft.

The US heavy bombers were the main recipients of the Me 262 attacks, but they were not the only ones. By this stage of the war Royal Air Force Bomber Command was mounting frequent daylight attacks on targets in Germany, and on the last day of March 460 Lancasters and Halifaxes set out to strike at the U-boat assembly yards at Hamburg. As they neared the target, Me 262s delivered a sharp attack which knocked down three Halifaxes and four Lancasters in rapid succession, before the escorts could drive them away.

At the same time, more than a thousand American heavy bombers were attacking Zeitz, Brandenburg, Brunswick and Halle, and these were also engaged by jet fighters. *JG 7* flew 38 sorties that day and, on the available evidence, it appears that the jets shot down fourteen enemy bombers and two fighters, for a loss of four of their number. That was the high-water mark of achievement for the Me 262 units, and it would never be surpassed. Yet, even on that most successful day, the losses inflicted by the jets amounted to only 1 per cent of the huge Allied forces involved. Despite the massive German exertion, the effect was no more than a pin-prick.

Early in April one further Me 262 fighter unit, *Jagdverband 44*, commanded by *Generalmajor* Adolf Galland in person, became operational at Munich/Riem. With many of the *Luftwaffe* piston-engine day-fighter units now grounded for want of fuel, Galland was able to draw into his unit several ace pilots, including Johannes Steinhoff, Günther Lützow, Heinz Bär and Gerhard Barkhorn. The unit flew its first interception mission on 5 April, when five fighters were scrambled and claimed the destruction of two enemy bombers. With Allied ground forces now advancing deep into Germany, however, the *Luftwaffe* fighter control organization was on its last legs. Even the uniquely talented pilots of *JV 44* were unable to achieve much: rarely would the unit fly more than half a dozen sorties or shoot down more than a couple of Allied aircraft in a day. Compared with the hugh Allied air activity, this was indeed a puny effort, and the appearance of *JV 44* passed unnoticed by its opponents.

On 7 April the Me 262 fighter force mounted its largest defensive effort, flying a total of 59 sorties. Owing to poor control, they failed to deliver a concentrated attack and they claimed only five Allied aircraft destroyed for the loss of two of their own. On 9 April, the last date for which figures are available, there were about 200 Me 262s on the strength of the various operational units. Of these, 163 were serving in the day-fighter role with *JG 7*, *KG(J) 54* and *JV 44*. *KG 51* possessed 21 fighter-bombers, there were about nine operating in the night-fighter role and seven were employed for tactical reconnaissance.

* * *

The last major air action involving Me 262s took place on 10 April 1945, when 55 of the jet fighters took off to engage more than 2,000 US heavy bombers and escorts attacking targets in the Berlin area. *Leutnant* Walther Hagenah flew with *III./JG 7* that day from Lärz near Berlin, with an inexperienced *Feldwebel* pilot as wingman:

Once above cloud at about 5,000m [16,250ft], I could see the bomber formation clearly, at about 6,000m [about 20,000ft]. I was flying at about 550km/h [340mph] in a shallow climb, and turned towards them. Then, as an experienced fighter pilot, I had that old 'tingling on the back of neck' that something was wrong. I scanned the sky and, ahead and high above, I caught sight of six Mustangs passing above from almost head-on. At first I thought they had not seen me, and [I] continued towards the bombers. But to be on the safe side I glanced back, and it was a good thing that I did, because the Mustangs were curving round and diving on the pair of us.

Mustangs in the dive the were considerably faster than the jet fighters in the climb, and the piston-engine fighters soon reached firing range. Tracers flashed disconcertingly close in front of Hagenah's aircraft:

> I lowered my nose slightly to increase speed and resolved to try to outrun the Mustangs. I did not attempt any manoeuvre to throw off their aim; I knew that the moment I turned, my speed would fall and then they would have me. I told the *Feldwebel* with me to keep going, but obviously he was scared of the tracers because I saw him weaving from side to side, then he broke away to the left. That was just what the Mustang pilots wanted and in no time they were on to him. His aircraft received several hits and I saw it go down and crash.

Hagenah used his speed advantage to outdistance the Mustangs and he saw the enemy fighters turn away to the west. He had sufficient fuel for a retaliatory attack so he turned after them and quickly caught up. Hagenah opened fire and thought he hit a Mustang, then, maintaining his speed, he broke off the action and dived away to return to base.

That day Me 262s claimed the destruction of ten B-17s and seven escorts. These claims find general support in US records. In their turn, however, the jet fighters suffered their worst losses ever. Twenty-seven Me 262s were destroyed, nearly half of those committed. Far more serious than this loss in aircraft—which could be replaced—was the loss of nineteen irreplaceable jet-fighter pilots killed and five wounded.

Now Allied troops were thrusting even more deeply into Germany: on 10 April American troops were nearing Nuremberg and the Red Army was within 60 miles of Berlin. As jet-fighter bases were overrun one by one, the operations by these aircraft underwent a rapid decline, and by the end of the month they had virtually ceased.

* * *

In retrospect, it is clear that Hitler's edict regarding the use of the Me 262 as a fighter-bomber caused no appreciable delay in the type's operational introduction in the fighter role. Nor can the *Luftwaffe* reasonably be censured for not rushing the aircraft into production soon enough. Indeed, if anything, production was initiated too soon, for Me 262 airframes started to come off the assembly lines several months before the Jumo 004 engine that powered it was ready for mass production. As we have seen, the failure of the Me 262 in action had much more to do with its unreliable new powerplant, coupled with the direct and indirect pressures imposed by the Allied air attacks, than to shortcomings on the part of the German leadership.

By the beginning of April 1945 the *Luftwaffe* had taken delivery of more than 1,200 Me 262s. Yet there were never more than 200 of these aircraft in service with combat units. During the final months of the war, the *Luftwaffe* faced such intractable problems that its fighter units were quite unable to exploit the superior performance of the Me 262. In combat they suffered heavy losses and achieved little. Given the numerical superiority and the quality of the forces arraigned against them, it could hardly have been otherwise.

CHAPTER THIRTEEN

Furball over Hai Duong

The air war over North Vietnam lasted from August 1964 to January 1973 and was the first conflict in which surface-to-air and air-to-air guided missiles played a leading role. With the advent of the missile-armed supersonic fighter, many people believed that the dogfight—the close-quarter combat involving several aircraft—was a thing of the past. In the case of the great majority of engagements, they were right: given any choice in the matter, the pilot with the higher-performance fighter and the better weapons system would seek to open the range and proceed to pick off enemy planes with missiles from beyond the reach of any return fire. But circumstances can force pilots to engage in a dogfight whether they want to or not. That happened over North Vietnam, on one day during the spring of 1972.

DURING THE US air campaign against North Vietnam, one air-to-air action stands out as being the most concentrated of all, in terms of the number of aircraft involved and the small volume of sky in which it occurred—that between US carrier planes and North Vietnamese MiG fighters in the afternoon of 10 May 1972, above the provincial town of Hai Duong.

At that time the US Navy had three aircraft carriers on station off the coast of North Vietnam, positioned to deliver air strikes on targets in that country—*Constellation* and *Kitty Hawk*, each displacing 74,000 tons, and the smaller *Coral Sea*, displacing 49,000 tons. During the morning of 10 May the carrier planes hit targets around the port of Haiphong. Shortly before noon, the three carriers launched their second air strikes of the day, against targets around Hai Duong some 30 miles east of Hanoi. *Constellation*'s A-6s and A-7s were to hit the railway marshalling yard; those from *Kitty Hawk* and *Coral Sea* were to hit road and rail bridges nearby.

Carrier Air Wing 9 from *Constellation* led the attack, its aircraft comprising six Grumman A-6 Intruders, each carrying sixteen 500lb bombs; ten Vought A-7 Corsairs, each carrying twelve 500lb bombs; eight McDonnell F-4 Phantoms flying as escorts, each carrying four Sparrow (radar guided) and four Sidewinder (infra-red homing) air-to-air missiles; four F-4s configured for both flak-suppression and escort, each carrying six Rockeye cluster bombs, four Sidewinder and two Sparrow air-to-air missiles; two A-7s configured for the 'Iron Hand' missile-suppression role, each carrying two Shrike radar-homing missiles and six cluster bombs; one North American RA-5C Vigilante reconnaissance aircraft to take post-strike photographs of the target; and one Douglas EKA-3B Skywarrior to jam enemy long-range radars (this plane also operated in the tanker role and could provide fuel to other aircraft in the force that required it). The Air Wing flew at 15,000ft and headed for the mouth of the Red River, the other two Air Wings following at ten-minute intervals with a separation of about 60 miles between each.

At 12.54 p.m. *Constellation*'s Air Wing crossed the coast of North Vietnam and turned on to a north-westerly heading for Hai Duong. As the formation neared the zone defended by surface-to-air missiles (SAMs), the single EKA-3B Skywarrior climbed to 20,000ft and began flying an oblong orbit pattern. At the briefed time the crew switched on their transmitters to jam the enemy radar frequencies.

In each of the attacking planes the crew methodically scanned the sky around them for the tell-tale muzzle or rocket flash or the glint of sun that might be the first sign of an enemy attack. If the enemy fighters, shells or missiles were to be avoided, it was essential to begin an evasive manoeuvre in good time. The men knew that their lives depended on the efficiency of the search. Radar and radar warning receivers were useful aids, but it would have been foolhardy to place one's trust in those alone.

As it neared the target, the formation split into its component parts, which moved to their allotted places. The two 'Iron Hand' A-7s and their escorting Phantoms headed for positions on either side of the target, ready to engage any enemy SAM control radars that came on the air. The Phantom escorts made for patrol lines to the north, east and west of the target, ready to block the paths of possible incoming MiGs. The A-6s and A-7s headed for separate points to the north of the target, from which they were to roll into their attack dives.

From his Phantom cockpit, Lieutenant Randy Cunningham, part of the flak-suppression force, watched the A-6s and A-7s deliver their attacks on the marshalling yard. Shell-bursts pock-marked the sky, but the American pilot did not notice any muzzle flashes to betray the positions of the guns he was supposed to attack. He and his wingman dropped their cluster bombs on their secondary target, a group of warehouses beside the rail yard. After he had released his bombs, Cunningham pulled out of the dive, and his back-seater Willie Driscoll glanced back at the target. Just above the horizon, to his left, he noticed several black dots in the sky. It took a few seconds to work out that they were planes, then that they were MiG-17s. The sudden arrival of the enemy fighters caught Cunningham off guard, at the time he was in a starboard turn concentrating his attention on seeing where his bombs had landed:

> I shouldn't have been doing that: I wasn't thinking about MiGs. I reversed port and saw two MiG-17s slashing in with guns going, inside gun range. I don't know why they didn't hit me: I could see tracers flying by the canopy.

The MiG was closing in fast and Cunningham could see that its pilot was hauling on the stick to bring his gun sight to bear, so the American turned sharply into the attack and forced the enemy fighter to overshoot. He then reversed his turn and the enemy wingman also shot past him. Now Cunningham could deliver his counter-attack. He reversed course, aligned his sight on one of the MiGs and squeezed the trigger. Trailing smoke, the Sidewinder streaked after the North

---

McDONNELL F-4J PHANTOM

Role: Two-seat, carrier-based, multi-role fighter.

Power: Two General Electric J79-GE-10 turbojet engines each developing 17,900lb of thrust with afterburning.

Armament: (Fighter role) Four AIM-7E Sparrow semi-active radar missiles and four AIM-9G Sidewinder infra-red homing missiles; (air-to-ground role during 10 May 1972 action) ten 500lb Rockeye cluster bombs plus a self-protection armament of two AIM-7E and four AIM-9G missiles.

Performance: Maximum speed (clean) 1,430mph (Mach 2.17) at 36,000ft; maximum rate of climb (clean) 49,800ft/min.

Normal operational take-off weight: 53,000lb.

Dimensions: Span 38ft 4in; length 63ft; wing area 530 sq ft.

Date of first production F-4J: December 1966.

Vietnamese fighter in a shallow left turn, then it smashed into the MiG, which exploded into a ball of fire.

Cunningham had no time to savour the victory, for a quick glance behind revealed yet another MiG-17 trying to close to within firing range. He increased speed and turned to drag the enemy plane in front of his wingman, Brian Grant, to give the latter an easy missile shot. But Grant had problems of his own, with another MiG-17 behind him and shooting when its pilot could bring the gun sight to bear. Taking in the situation, Cunningham saw that the only safe way out was to make use of the Phantom's greatly superior acceleration compared with the Soviet-built enemy fighters. Selecting full afterburner, the two American pilots surged away from their pursuers.

Despite of the efforts of the escorting Phantoms to drive them off, some of the North Vietnamese fighters succeeded in reaching the A-6s and A-7s now speeding for the coast. Circling over the target at 18,000ft in his Phantom, Lieutenant Matt Connelly observed an A-7 being chased by a couple of enemy fighters. He rolled his aircraft into a diving turn, aligned his nose on one of the MiG-17s and loosed off a Sidewinder. The North Vietnamese pilot saw the missile coming and broke away sharply to avoid it, but in forcing the enemy fighter to abandon its attack on the A-7 the missile had done its job.

As he came away from the target, A-7 pilot Lieutenant Al Junker lost contact with his element leader. He searched the sky around for friendly planes to join up with, and saw what looked like an A-6 heading towards him:

> A few seconds later I looked back again to see how he was coming along and saw red dots coming from each side of his nose. A-6s did not have guns, and even if they did they would not be shooting at me—it was a MiG-17!

Junker pulled into a hard turn to avoid the enemy fire and saw the cannon shells streak past his left wing, so close that he felt their shock waves.

Meanwhile Junker's element leader, Commander Fred Baldwin, had seen that his wingman was in trouble and turned to go to his assistance. Baldwin barrel-rolled into a firing position behind the North Vietnamese fighter. From there he could threaten the enemy plane, but, lacking missiles and with his single 20mm cannon unserviceable, that was all he could do. Of course, the enemy pilot had no way of knowing that the A-7 behind him was unarmed, and each time Baldwin moved into a firing position the MiG broke off its attack.

The high-speed slalom over the paddy fields had been in progress for several miles when another A-7 pilot, Lieutenant George Goryanec, joined the fight:

> I turned and saw them behind me: they were a lot lower than I was. I could see Al Junker with an airplane behind him and Fred Baldwin, a couple of thousand feet off to one side, calling the turns. What looked like a line of 'grapefruits' was going past Al's nose. That made me mad—the guy was trying to shoot Al down.

Goryanec's aircraft had a serviceable cannon, and he could play a more active role in assisting his comrade. He rolled the A-7 on its back and curved after the MiG, aligning himself for an attack from above. He fired a long burst at the enemy plane and saw what looked like a couple of hits near the wing root. Goryanec broke off his attack, looked back to see what the MiG was doing and observed that the latter had broken off and was heading north, away from the fight. Thanks to the timely intervention of the two A-7s, Al Junker's plane had survived the engagement without taking any damage.

Matt Connelly joined the mêlée after his spoiling attack on the MiG-17 and aligned the nose of his Phantom on another of the enemy fighters. In his headphones he heard a buzz to denote that the Sidewinder had locked on to the heat source, but the MiG was in a tight turn and he knew that there was little chance of hitting it. If the MiG pilot had held his turn he would have escaped, but perhaps he panicked at the sight of the Phantom bounding towards him. The North Vietnamese pilot made the tactical blunder of rolling out of the turn at that point, presenting Connelly with the opportunity of a snap shot. From about 400yds—almost at minimum range—he launched a Sidewinder and watched it detonate close to the enemy fighter's tail. The rear of the plane exploded, and moments later its pilot ejected.

Having shaken off the MiGs that had been chasing them, Randy Cunningham and Brian Grant converted their excess speed into altitude and took their Phantoms up to 12,000ft in a fast zoom-climb. Then both pilots turned to assess the dogfight taking place far below. Close to the ground they saw no fewer than eight MiG-17s flying in a loose defensive circle, each covering the tail of the one in front. The two Phantoms were in a perfect position to attack the enemy fighters from above, and their pilots entered diving turns to position themselves to deliver a missile attack.

Matters closer to hand brought an end to this plan, however. Suddenly a Phantom flashed past Cunningham's nose, so close that it nearly collided with him. The aircraft belonged to Commander Dwight Timm, who was under co-ordinated attack from three MiGs. A MiG-17 was about 1,000yds behind him and firing, and a MiG-21 was following him a little further behind, awaiting its chance to engage. Timm was turning tightly to port to avoid their fire, but in the process he failed to see the greatest threat of all—a MiG-17 only 100yds away from him, hidden under his wing and edging into a firing position.

As Timm and his pursuers sped past, Cunningham pulled his aircraft into a tight turn to go to his friend's assistance. He placed his gun sight over the MiG that posed the greatest threat to Timm and prepared to launch a Sidewinder, but he knew that the heat-seeking missile had to be used with great caution in a close-quarter dogfight such as this. The missile could not tell friend from foe: it merely homed on to the strongest heat source within its field of view—which would probably be the jet pipes of Timm's aircraft. Cunningham shouted to Timm to reverse his turn and go starboard, and as the Phantom swung clear he squeezed off the Sidewinder. The missile exploded against the tail of the enemy fighter, which wallowed drunkenly, and its pilot ejected. On seeing that, one MiG broke off its chase and Timm accelerated clear of the other.

Having already knocked down one MiG-17, Matt Connelly was curving into position to engage another. And this North Vietnamese pilot reacted in exactly the same way as Connelly's first victim:

> The guy did the same thing: he saw me coming and started turning. I went behind him, he reversed his turn and I pulled back behind him. I waited till I had a real good tone, but as I squeezed the trigger the tone dropped off.

At first Connelly thought the missile was a dud, but then it appeared to sort itself out and it continued relentlessly after the enemy fighter. The weapon exploded beside MiG and blew away part of the tail, causing the aircraft to enter a fast roll to the left and the pilot to eject.

Circling in their Phantoms at 14,000ft, Commander Harry Blackburn and his wingman were patrolling some distance away from the main dogfight, positioned to intercept any MiG that attempted to enter or leave the fight. Steve Rudloff, Blackburn's back-seater, made a radar search for MiGs but found none within the set's angle of view. He returned his attention to a search of the sides and rear outside the cockpit, and at that instant several black smoke clouds appeared between him and his wingman—the pair were being engaged by 85mm guns. A moment later Rudloff felt the Phantom shudder as one of the 20lb shells exploded close to its tail. Although he was strapped tightly into his seat, the radar operator was thrown hard against the side of the cockpit. He was in the process of collecting his senses when the instrument panel in front of him suddenly erupted into a mass of smoke and flame. A glance in the rear-view mirrors revealed that the rear of the plane was also on fire.

Then something in front of Rudloff exploded with a dazzling white flash. In a split second his natural reflexes had pressed shut his eyelids, but that was too long. When he next opened his eyes he could see nothing: the flash had blinded him. The plane was obviously beyond saving and Blackburn gave the order to eject. Rudloff yanked the firing handle, there was a deafening roar as the seat fired and he felt a tumbling sensation. Then everything went quiet as his parachute brought him slowly to the ground. Rudloff was taken prisoner immediately

---

MIKOYAN-GUREVICH MiG-17 ('FRESCO')

Role: Single-seat day fighter.
Power: One Klimov VK-1 turbojet developing 7,500lb of thrust with afterburning.
Armament: Three NR-23 23mm cannon.
Performance: Maximum speed 710mph at 10,000ft; maximum rate of climb 12,795ft/min.
Normal operational take-off weight: 14,750lb
Dimensions: Span 31ft 7in; length 36ft 4¼in; wing area 243.3 sq ft.
Date of first production MiG-17: October 1952.

---

after landing, and his sight would return in stages over the next couple of hours. Harry Blackburn, his pilot, also ejected but would later die in captivity.

Meanwhile the air action above Hai Duong continued with unabated fury. Lieutenant Steve Shoemaker aligned his Phantom on another of the enemy fighters and Lieutenant Keith Crenshaw, his back-seater, recalled:

> We came on this MiG-17 to the south-west of the 'furball'. He appeared in front of us; he seemed to be trying to get out of the fight. We didn't make any big turn: we dived on him and I heard 'Shoe' call, 'We got a good [missile] tone', then he fired the Sidewinder.

The Phantom's dive was taking it close to the ground, and the pilot was forced to pull up sharply, with the result that the MiG passed out of sight. Once established in the climb, Shoemaker rolled his fighter on its side and the two Americans observed thick, black, greasy smoke rising from the point on the ground where the enemy fighter had crashed.

By now all of the A-6s and A-7s were safely clear of the target and the Air Group Leader, Commander Gus Eggert, ordered the escorting fighters to break off the action and head back for the carrier. On his way to the coast, Randy Cunningham noticed a plane some distance in front, end-on and apparently stationary. The silhouette increased in size, then the high-set tailplane betrayed it as yet another MiG-17:

> I tried to meet this guy head-on, and all of a sudden he opened fire with tracer. I pulled straight up into the vertical, going up through 15,000 feet, pulled 6Gs going over the top. I looked back, I expected to see him moving straight through and running. But we were canopy to canopy, maybe 400 or 500 feet apart!

Cunningham rolled on his back at the top of the climb and saw his opponent loose off a burst of cannon fire in his direction. Then, as the Phantom dived away, the MiG slid into position behind it—obviously this enemy pilot was no novice at air fighting. Cunningham continued:

> I pitched my nose up, pulled over the top, and rolled in behind his 6 o'clock. As soon as I dropped my nose he pulled straight up into the vertical again. I overshot, he rolled up over the top, pulled through and rolled in behind me.

In turn, each pilot pulled up and rolled into position behind his opponent, to seize a marginal advantage over his opponent. So long as the process continued, neither pilot could get into a firing position, but Cunningham knew he could not let it continue for long. Throughout the low-altitude manoeuvring both planes were losing speed, and in a low-speed fight the MiG 17 could outmanoeuvre the Phantom. During his 'Top Gun' course, Cunningham had practised just the manoeuvre to disentangle him from such a situation:

> The MiG was sitting at my 7 o'clock. When he got his nose just a little too high, I pulled sharply down into him and met him head on. Then I lit the burners and accelerated away from him. By the time he got his nose on me I was about a mile and a half ahead of him, out of [cannon] firing range and opening.

Cunningham then pulled into another vertical climb to move into a firing position. To his surprise, the MiG again followed him. He had never encountered an enemy pilot who was so aggressive or who had such a grasp of air-fighting tactics. The American pilot broke out of the clinch as before and pulled into yet another zoom climb, and yet again the MiG followed. This time Cunningham decided to try something different. As the two fighters clawed for altitude, flying almost canopy to canopy, he pulled the throttles to idle and opened the speed brakes. The Phantom decelerated rapidly and the MiG sped out in front. Then Cunningham closed the speed brakes and selected full afterburner:

> I think that caught him by surprise because he shot way out in front of me. But a Phantom on full afterburner at 150 knots with the nose straight up in the air is not really flying, it is standing on 36,000 pounds of thrust. We were hanging behind him but we were not really in a position of advantage. At those speeds a MiG-17 had about 2½ to 3 more Gs available than we had.

As the MiG reached the top of its climb, Cunningham applied full rudder and pulled underneath his opponent. The MiG rolled on to its back, then headed for the ground.

Perhaps the North Vietnamese pilot was running short of fuel and was trying to break out of the fight. Whatever the reason, he made the fundamental error of presenting his tail to Cunningham. The American pilot curved into a firing position, placed the gun sight pipper over the MiG and squeezed the trigger. The Sidewinder's smoke trail reached out to the enemy fighter and detonated a few yards away from it, but caused no apparent damage. The MiG continued its fast-diving turn, making no attempt to pull out, however, and a few moments later it smashed into the ground and exploded.

It was six minutes since Cunningham and Driscoll had first seen the MiGs sweeping in towards Hai Duong, and during the furious action six MiG-17s had been destroyed and one probably damaged; one Phantom had been shot down by ground fire and another was seriously damaged. In time and space the action was the most concentrated ever fought over North Vietnam, and it was not over yet.

Heading for the coast in a climb, Cunningham and his back-seater were elated at having shot down three enemy planes during the short action. During previous weeks they had shot down two MiGs, so their score now stood at five—they had gained the coveted status of fighter aces. Then, suddenly and without warning as the Phantom passed through 16,000ft, a surface-to-air missile exploded within 200yds of the aircraft. The blast hurled the fighter into a steep bank and splinters from the warhead tore into the plane. Cunningham levelled out, looked for signs of obvious damage but saw none. He checked his instruments and, as everything seemed to be in order, continued the climb. The aircraft handled normally and it looked as if it had escaped with a minor shaking.

It had not. Just over a minute later, as the Phantom climbed through 27,000ft, it gave an lurch and the port wing dropped. Again the pilot checked his instruments and this time he saw that the pressure gauge for the main hydraulic system read zero and that for the secondary system was falling. It was clear that the hydraulic system had been ruptured and the precious fluid was seeping away.

The Phantom depended on hydraulic pressure to drive its flying controls, and as the oil pressure dropped away the control systems failed one by one. The first sign of this was when the leading edge of the tailplane edged into the fully down position, forcing the plane's nose up. The text-book answer for pilots in that situation was simple: eject immediately. But the plane was still over North Vietnam: if the men bailed out now they were almost certain to be taken prisoner. Their only hope of avoiding that fate lay in staying with their plane and keeping it in the air just a little longer. If they could reach the coast and parachute into the sea, the chances of rescue would be immeasurably greater.

Cunningham had heard how another pilot in a similar situation had brought his Phantom out of North Vietnam. Following his example, Cunningham now pressed hard on the right rudder pedal to use some of the remaining hydraulic pressure to push the fighter into a yaw to the right. The plane's nose fell and it rolled to the right. As the nose passed through the horizontal, Cunningham pulled back the throttles and extended the speed brakes to prevent the plane from entering a dive. Then the pilot pushed on left rudder, selected full power and retracted the speed brakes. The Phantom continued to roll through 360 degrees until it was the right way up, then the nose pitched up again and Cunningham repeated the process. The Phantom flew a series of extremely clumsy barrel rolls, each one of which carried the stricken aircraft a little closer to the coast and relative safety.

Meanwhile, terrible things were happening at the rear of the fighter. A fire had broken out and the flames rapidly took hold. Then came a small explosion, which deprived Cunningham of the last vestiges of control over the aircraft. The nose pitched up for the last time, then it dropped and the fighter fell into an inverted spin. The doughty pilot was reluctant to leave the crippled fighter, but he was forced to admit defeat. He told Driscoll to eject, then he followed.

In its death throes, the Phantom had performed the final task demanded of it: as the pair dangled from their parachutes they saw plenty of beautiful water below them. Shortly after they splashed into the sea, both men were picked up by rescue helicopters.

Afterwards it was assessed that the twelve Phantoms of *Constellation*'s Air Wing had engaged about twenty North Vietnamese fighters—fourteen MiG-17s, two MiG-19s and four MiG-21s. Six MiG-17s had been shot down. During the engagement, ten Sidewinder and three Sparrow air-to-air missiles had been fired, giving an average of just over two missiles fired per aircraft shot down. Air aces are not subject to the law of averages, however, and in his exemplary performance Randy Cunningham had destroyed three enemy fighters for an expenditure of just three Sidewinders. One MiG-17 was assessed as probably damaged by cannon fire from an A-7. During the action two Phantoms had been lost, one to a SAM and one to ground fire, and a Phantom was seriously damaged by ground fire.

* * *

Had the Phantoms not had other aircraft to protect, their correct tactic would have been to accelerate away from the MiGs, climb above their adversaries and then deliver a series of long-range attacks with missiles to pick off the enemy planes. But the Phantoms' primary duty was to protect the A-6s and A-7s, and that requirement forced them into the dogfight. On the other hand, Randy Cunningham's close-quarter, manoeuvring fight with the MiG-17 was an aberration. He did not have to enter that fight, and by engaging the more manoeuvrable enemy fighter on its own terms he forfeited the Phantom's advantages of superior speed and superior long-range weaponry. Thanks to the Phantom's better acceleration, however, he knew that he could always break out of the fight whenever he chose. His opponent fought unexpectedly well, but the lower-performance MiG-17 did not allow the option of a safe exit. This proved to be its undoing, and when the North Vietnamese pilot turned away he presented Cunningham with an easy missile shot. The American pilot made the most of the unexpected opportunity. As William Sholto Douglas had stressed more than half a century earlier, if one entered a combat it was valuable to have the means of breaking out of it cleanly if things got too hot.

CHAPTER FOURTEEN

Low Level Drama in front of San Carlos

*At the start of a conflict, aerial warfare is a 'come-as-you-are' business, in which
resourceful men have often to go into action with aircraft that have
been designed for a quite different purpose. If the conflict is of brief duration,
there will be insufficient time to introduce equipment tailored to their needs.
A classic example of this phenomenon occurred in the spring of 1982, when
Great Britain and Argentina came into conflict over the possession of the
Falkland Islands.*

WHEN THE BRITISH GOVERNMENT decided to send a naval task force to
the South Atlantic to retake the Falkland Islands, the fighter protection for the
planned amphibious landing operation rested upon what could be achieved by a
couple of dozen British Aerospace Sea Harrier aircraft. This short-range, subsonic, VSTOL (vertical and short take-off and landing) machine was a low-cost
adaptation of the RAF ground-attack Harrier. The Royal Navy had ordered the
aircraft as a general-purpose, carrier-based fighter to support naval operations far
out to sea where, it was anticipated, it would be beyond the reach of enemy
high-performance, land-based fighters. Although the Sea Harrier was equipped
for air-to-air combat, in this role its primary targets were to be the large and relatively slow maritime reconnaissance aircraft used to shadow naval forces and
guide in attacking aircraft.

In the context of the Falklands conflict, the Sea Harriers had a much lower
maximum speed than the Argentine-operated Mirages and Daggers and the British fighters were outnumbered three to one by these and the enemy Skyhawks and
Super Etendards. Set against these drawbacks, however, the Sea Harrier pilots enjoyed three important advantages over their opponents. The first concerned the
main air-to-air weapon carried by their aircraft, the AIM-9L Sidewinder. This, the
latest variant of the famous infra-red missile, was more reliable, was longer-rang-
ing, had a wider engagement envelope and was generally much more effective
than the French and Israeli air-to-air missiles carried by Argentine aircraft. The
second advantage concerned the Sea Harrier pilots' level of training. The Fleet
Air Arm had the full use of NATO training facilities and its air-fighting doctrines
were based on the lessons learned during every previous conflict up to and including that in Vietnam. Prior to the Falklands conflict, the Argentine Air Force and
Navy had never engaged in air-to-air combat, and their pilots had no effective
tactical doctrine for engaging enemy fighters. The third advantage enjoyed by the
British pilots resulted from the unique VSTOL capability of their aircraft. The
much-published ability to 'viff' (vector thrust in forward flight) enabled them to
tighten turns to a degree impossible for conventional fighter types. Moreover, al-

though it was subsonic in level flight, once it had burned some of its fuel the Sea Harrier had a thrust-to-weight ratio close to unity and its acceleration and climbing performance were vastly better than those of its opponents. The value of these attributes lay in their morale effect on the Argentine pilots: the latter knew of the Sea Harrier's unusual manoeuvring capabilities and were reluctant to enter a close-quarter fight where they could expect to be at a disadvantage. But nor could they engage the Sea Harriers at long range with any prospect of success, because of the latter's superior missile armament.

* * *

The air war over the Falklands opened on 1 May 1982. Taking a show of force off the islands by Royal Navy warships as the prelude to the expected landing operation, the Argentine Air Force flew 56 fighter, fighter-bomber and bomber sorties into the area. In the course of the aerial skirmishes that followed, the Sea Harriers shot down a Canberra, a Dagger and a Mirage without loss to themselves. Another Mirage suffered damage and, as it was about to make an emergency landing on Port Stanley airfield, it was shot down by Argentine anti-aircraft gunners.

Following this engagement, the Argentine High Command maintained a limited pressure against the British Task Force, intending to conserve its strength until the real amphibious landings took place. Then there would be plenty of high-value targets off the coast and it would remain to be seen whether the Sea Harriers and their covering warships could prevent attacking aircraft from inflicting heavy casualties.

* * *

The British landings on the Falklands began during the early morning darkness of 21 May. Then, following a small reinforcement to make up for losses, the Task Force had 25 Sea Harriers, split between No 800 Squadron in HMS *Hermes* and No 801 Squadron in *Invincible*. The Argentine Air Force and Naval Air units arrayed against them possessed about 75 jet fighters and fighter-bombers.

San Carlos Water, the site chosen for the landings, lies at the north-western tip of East Falkland. The inlet runs north to south, is just over a mile wide and four miles long and is deep enough to accommodate large ships. For ships seeking to avoid air attack, the inlet has the attributes of a slit trench: it is surrounded by hills on all sides except the south-east and the entrance at the north-west. Because of this topography, aircraft engaged in low-altitude attacks would have to make their bombing runs along the north–south axis of the waterway, in one direction or the other.

Although small by Second World War standards, the landing at San Carlos was still a sizeable undertaking. The troops and their equipment were carried to the inlet aboard twelve transports, escorted by a guided missile destroyer and six frigates. Once the transports reached their assigned positions in the inlet, they dropped anchor and began off-loading, with landing craft and helicopters running a shuttle service to the shore. The escorting warships, with the exception of a frigate positioned across the entrance to San Carlos Water, were disposed outside the waterway in readiness to ward off enemy counter-attacks that could not be long in coming.

Soon after dawn the British carriers began sending off pairs of fighters in relays, to protect the landing area. The enemy fighter-bombers were certain to attack at low altitude, below the cover of the British ships' radars and their long-range missiles. Lacking the assistance of airborne early-warning radar, the Sea Harriers' tactics can best be described as 'pre-Battle of Britain'. They mounted standing patrols at two points, one near Pebble Island and the other half way down Falkland Sound, respectively to the north-west and the south-west of the landing area and about 30 miles from it. The Sea Harrier's simple pulsed radar was useless against aircraft flying at low altitude over land, so the pilots had to search visually for the incoming enemy planes.

At thirty-minute intervals a fresh pair of Sea Harriers arrived at one of the patrol areas, and remained in position for 10–15 minutes. It would, of course, have been better if they could have stayed longer, but the Royal Navy carriers were themselves under threat from Super Etendard aircraft carrying Exocet missiles and this forced them to remain at least 200 miles to the east of the Islands. As a means of protecting the landings, the air defence plan was far from watertight. Both in time and in space there were gaps through which low-flying enemy fighter-bombers could penetrate to the landing area. Then it would be up to the ships' own missile and gun defences to deter enemy pilots from making accurate attacks or, if that deterrence failed, shoot them down.

The first Argentine aircraft to approach San Carlos never reached the inlet. Captain Jorge Benitez, flying a twin-engine Pucará light attack aircraft of *Grupo 3* on a routine reconnaissance mission from Goose Green airfield, had the misfortune to pass low over a British Army special forces patrol south of the waterway. One of the men fired a shoulder-launched Stinger infra-red missile at the plane, which homed on an engine exhaust and detonated. The Argentine pilot was forced to eject and the aircraft crashed.

BRITISH AEROSPACE SEA HARRIER FRS Mk 1

Role: Single-seat, carrier-based, general-purpose fighter.

Power: One Rolls-Royce Pegasus 104 vectored-thrust, turbofan engine developing 21,500lb of thrust.

Armament: Two ADEN 30mm cannon; (air-to-air role) two AIM-9L Sidewinder infra-red homing missiles; (air-to-ground role) two 1,000lb bombs or two 640lb BL755 cluster bomb units.

Performance: Maximum speed (clean) 736mph (Mach 0.91) at low altitude; climb to 40,000ft, 2min 23sec.

Normal operational take-off weight: 26,200lb.

Dimensions: Span 25ft 3in; length 47ft 7in; wing area 201.1 sq ft.

Date of first production Sea Harrier: August 1978.

Early that morning the Argentine Army headquarters at Port Stanley received a report that British warships had entered the northern end of Falkland Sound and were bombarding the coastline. This was thought to be yet another diversionary attack. Not until 10 a.m. did another Pucará on reconnaissance get through to observe what was happening at San Carlos. Its pilot reported that there were twelve enemy ships in the inlet, some of which were unloading troops and equipment.

The first air attack on the ships followed a few minutes later, delivered by a Macchi 339 light attack aircraft of the 1st Naval Attack *Escuadrilla*. Lieutenant Owen Crippa, flying on an armed reconnaissance mission from Port Stanley, swept low over the hills surrounding San Carlos Water and suddenly found himself over the beach-head. Braving the return fire, Crippa attacked the frigate *Argonaut* with four 5in rockets and 30mm cannon fire, causing minor damage to the ship and wounding three of the crew.

About half an hour later, at 10.35 a.m., the first fighter-bombers arrived from the mainland. At the head of six Daggers of *Grupo 6*, Major Carlos Martinez was to carry out an armed reconnaissance of the reported landing area. The Daggers swept in from the north, avoiding the Sea Harriers patrolling over Pebble Island. The Argentine pilots caught sight of the three warships in position outside the waterway, and the force split up to attack them. Martinez ran in to bomb HMS *Broadsword*, Captain Rodhe and Lieutenant Bean went for *Argonaut* and Captain Moreno led the second section of three aircraft against HMS *Antrim*. The Daggers attacked with 1,000lb bombs and 30mm cannon and the warships replied with guns of all calibres and air-defence missiles. Bean's aircraft was hit by a Seacat missile, believed to have been fired from the frigate *Plymouth*, and crashed into the sea. The remaining Daggers ran out to the south, hotly pursued by a couple of Sea Harriers. But the Argentine planes, freed of their bombs, rapidly picked up speed and soon outdistanced the slower jump-jets.

The only ship to suffer serious damage was the destroyer *Antrim*, struck on the stern by a 1,000lb bomb. The weapon went clean through the missile loading doors, narrowly missing a fully armed Seaslug missile, before coming to rest in a lavatory area. Fortunately for the ship's crew, the weapon failed to explode. The warship also took about forty hits from cannon shells, which left two of the crew seriously wounded. The frigate *Broadsword* was also strafed, and suffered four casualties. Following the attack, *Antrim* moved into San Carlos Water, where a bomb-disposal team defused the bomb and removed it.

Shortly before noon, Major Juan Tomba of *Grupo 3* led a pair of Pucarás from Goose Green to attack the beach-head. A patrol of three Sea Harriers from No 801 Squadron was on the point of returning to *Invincible* when the air controller informed the leader, Lieutenant-Commander 'Sharkey' Ward, of the enemy aircraft flying to the south of San Carlos Water. As the trio passed over the area at 15,000ft, Lieutenant Steve Thomas caught sight of one of the Pucarás. He and Lieutenant-Commander Al Craig dived on the machine, Tomba's, to attack with cannon. The jet fighters' overtaking speed was too great, however, and both pilots overshot the target without scoring hits. While they were thus engaged, the second Pucará escaped. Then Ward ran in to attack Tomba's aircraft with cannon. He scored hits on one of his opponent's wings, before he also overshot the slow Pucará. Having gauged the speed of the enemy plane, Ward lowered his flaps and went in for his second attack much more slowly:

> I opened fire and hit his right engine, which caught fire, and I saw bits falling off the aircraft. On my third pass I got in behind nicely and opened fire and saw his left engine start to burn, part of his canopy fly away, and pieces fall off the fuselage. I pulled away to the left thinking, this is incredible, he hasn't gone down yet! Then I saw the pilot eject. The aircraft continued on, hit the peat, and slid to a halt.

The next attacking force to set out from the mainland ran into difficulties from the outset. The four Skyhawks of *Grupo 5*, led by Captain Pablo Carballo, made their planned rendezvous with the KC-130 Hercules tanker aircraft off the coast of Argentina, but one could not take on fuel and had to turn back. Another went unserviceable and it, too, had to abandon the mission. The remaining two Skyhawks entered Falkland Sound, where they sighted a large merchant ship. It was the *Rio Carcarana*, an Argentine freighter used to supply the garrison on West Falkland, which was still drifting abandoned after being attacked by Sea Harriers five days earlier. Carballo lined up to attack the ship but at the last moment, unsure of its identity, he broke away. His wingman continued with the attack, released his bombs at the freighter and turned for home.

Alone, Carballo continued along the eastern side of Falkland Sound and suddenly came upon one of the British frigates. It was HMS *Ardent*, and her captain, Commander Alan West, later recalled:

> Suddenly somebody on the bridge shouted 'Aircraft closing!' and pointed. We looked in that direction and coming straight towards us from the south-west, over land, was a single Skyhawk about 4,000 yards away and closing very fast. He was right on the bow. I put on full wheel and called for full speed. As he flashed over us we were just beginning to turn, the 4.5-inch [gun] had no time to get on to him and the only thing that could fire was the 20mm. He dropped two bombs, one of which fell short and the other passed over us. He continued past us, banked round and flew down the Sound.

Lieutenant-Commanders Neil Thomas and Mike Blissett of No 800 Squadron had just arrived over Falkland Sound to start their patrol when the air controller ordered them to go after the aircraft that had attacked *Ardent*. The Sea Harriers descended below the puffs of cloud at 1,500ft and headed out over West Falkland. They failed to find Carballo's Skyhawk, but suddenly that became unimportant. As he passed about three miles east of Chartres Settlement, Blissett caught sight of four more Skyhawks in front of him and about 3½ miles away. The enemy planes, belonging to *Grupo 4*, had just crossed the coast on their way in. When their pilots sighted the Sea Harriers, they broke formation and jettisoned their bombs and underwing tanks, pulling hard to the right to avoid the attack. But by then the Sea Harriers were closing rapidly on the enemy planes, as Blissett later described:

I was in the lead with Neil to my left and about 400 yards astern, with all of us in a tight turn. The Skyhawks were in a long echelon, spread out over about a mile. I locked a Sidewinder on one of the guys in the middle and fired. My first impression was that the missile was going to strike the ground as it fell away—I was only about 200 feet above the ground. But suddenly it started to climb and rocketed towards the target. At that moment my attention was distracted somewhat as a Sidewinder came steaming past my left shoulder—Neil had fired past me, which I found very disconcerting at the time! I watched his 'Winder chase after another of the Skyhawks, which started to climb for a patch of cloud above, then the aircraft disappeared into the cloud with the missile gaining fast.

Blissett regaining his composure in time to see his missile strike the enemy plane, which blew up in a huge fireball. Seconds later another Skyhawk—the one he had last seen vanish into cloud chased by his wingman's Sidewinder—came tumbling from the sky above, out of control and with the fuselage ablaze. The surviving Skyhawks ran out to the west—fast. Lacking the fuel to continue after them, the Sea Harriers broke off the chase.

It was 2.30 p.m., the start of the most dangerous period for the British naval forces in and around San Carlos Water. Until now the Daggers and Skyhawks that reached the area had been engaged in armed reconnaissance missions, searching for the important targets and with time for only a snap attack if they found one. Three and a half hours had elapsed since the first mainland-based aircraft had flown over the area, and the pilots in the next attacking waves would know exactly where their targets lay and how they planned to engage them.

To meet the greater threat, the Sea Harrier patrols had been increased from two pairs of aircraft an hour to three pairs an hour. Lieutenant-Commander 'Fred' Frederiksen and Lieutenant Andy George of No 800 Squadron were on patrol when the next raiding forces—four Daggers of *Grupo 6*, led by Captain Horacio Gonzalez—swept in. One of the warships had observed the Argentine planes on radar before they descended to low altitude, however, and the controller ordered the Sea Harriers to move over West Falkland to intercept them. Flying at 2,500ft, Frederiksen caught sight of the raiders flying low, about three miles away to his

---

ISRAEL AIRCRAFT INDUSTRIES DAGGER

Role: Single-seat fighter-bomber.
Power: One Atar 9C turbojet engine developing 9,429lb of thrust with afterburner.
Armament: Two DEFA 30mm cannon; (air-to-air role) two IAI Shafrir infra-red homing missiles; (air-to-surface role over the Falklands) two 1,000lb bombs.
Performance: Maximum speed (clean, at low altitude) 830mph, (at 40,000ft) 1,460mph (Mach 2.2).
Normal operational take-off weight: 30,200lb.
Dimensions: Span 26ft 11in; length 51ft 0½in; wing area 376.7 sq ft.
Date of first production Dagger: Early 1972.
Note: This aircraft is an unlicensed, Israeli-built copy of the French Dassault Mirage V fighter-bomber.

---

right. He ordered his wingman into trail to watch out for possible escorts, and accelerated into position behind the left-hand pair of enemy planes. Frederiksen launched a Sidewinder and saw it home in and explode close to the tail of one of the Daggers. The fighter-bomber went into an uncontrolled roll and its pilot, Lieutenant Hector Luna, ejected just before it smashed into the ground. Luna's parachute did not open fully before he landed, and he suffered a dislocated arm and a sprained knee. Frederiksen loosed off with cannon at another of the Daggers, but he saw no hits before the enemy fighter-bombers vanished into the layer of cloud covering the ridge in front of them.

As this was happening, a new force of Skyhawks swung into Falkland Sound from the north. The six aircraft concentrated their attack on HMS *Argonaut* and hit her with two 1,000-pounders. One bomb smashed into her hull and demolished several steam pipes, causing a boiler to explode, then it went on to wreck part of the ship's steering gear. The other bomb impacted further forward and ended up in the forward Seacat magazine, where it caused two missiles to explode, killing two of the ship's crew. Although both bombs caused secondary explosions, the weapons had been released from too low an altitude for the fuses to function and neither weapon detonated.

Almost immediately afterwards the depleted Dagger formation from *Grupo* 6 sped over the coast of West Falkland and lined up to attack HMS *Ardent*. The aircraft were closing in rapidly from astern and Alan West called for full port rudder in a vain attempt to bring the ship's 4.5in gun to bear. For some reason the Seacat missile failed to leave its launcher at the critical time and the ship's only defences comprised a 20mm cannon and a few light machine guns. Running in to bomb the ship at the rear of the attacking force, Captain Robles watched the action begin:

> In front of Captain Gonzalez' plane we could see the tracers flashing towards us. His flight path took him between the masts of the frigate. His bomb hit the sea about 10 metres short of it and lifted a great mass of water which practically enveloped the ship; I believe the bomb skipped and embedded itself in the hull. Then Lieutenant Bernhardt released his bombs, one of which struck the upper part of the ship. Then I arrived at the release point and let go of my bombs.

With no effective defence to distract them, the Dagger pilots were able to press home an accurate attack. Alan West described what it felt like to be on the receiving end of their efforts:

> The first aircraft released two bombs, one of which hit us near the stern and went off. There was an enormous bang; it felt as if someone had got hold of the stern and was banging the ship up and down on the water. With the explosion a column of flash and smoke went up about 100 feet. I looked aft and saw the Seacat launcher about 20 feet in the air where it had been blown, and pieces of metal flying in all directions.

The bomb struck the frigate close to the helicopter hangar, blew off the roof and folded it over the starboard side, wrecking the ship's Lynx helicopter in the process. Several of the ship's crew were killed or injured. Another bomb embedded itself in the stern but failed to detonate.

If a warship has suffered damage in action there are three vital questions that her captain needs to answer: Can she stay afloat? Can she move under control? Can she continue to fight? As West received the damage reports from his First Lieutenant, it was clear that, although *Ardent* could float and move, she could not fight: the Seacat missile launcher had been blown overboard, and damage to the ammunition supply conveyor had put the 4.5in gun out of action too. As the damage-control teams worked to bring the fires under control, West headed for San Carlos Water, where his ship could receive protection from others in the force.

It was 2.45 p.m. and more Argentine planes were streaking over the waterway at low altitude to attack the British ships. HMS *Brilliant* suffered another strafing attack and had some of her crew were injured by flying splinters. Skyhawks entered San Carlos Water to attack the unloading transports, but their pilots found that the high ground surrounding the anchorage complicated the task. Ensign Marcelo Moroni of *Grupo 5* explained the problem:

> The topography of the island made it difficult to see into the bay because we were too low—we were so close to the hills we could not see over them. As we topped the last hill we saw eight or nine ships in the bay. The moment they saw us, they opened up at us with everything they had. Two of the Skyhawks went for one frigate, another two headed for another ship, and I was last of the five. Suddenly I felt a blow from my right and I thought my aircraft had been hit and damaged by enemy fire. Because of this I took no evasive action but headed straight towards my target; as soon as I dropped my bombs I continued on straight out of the bay.

Apart from one that suffered minor damage from small-arms fire, all the Skyhawks returned safely to Rio Gallegos. Moroni's aircraft was not hit; almost certainly he had run into the slipstream from one of the aircraft in front. No transports were hit.

While this was happening, a sharp engagement was taking place over West Falkland. On their second patrol of the day, 'Sharkey' Ward and Steve Thomas were at the southern end of their orbit when the latter noticed a pair of low-flying Daggers heading east:

> I barrelled in behind them, locked up a missile on the rear guy and fired. The Sidewinder hit the aircraft and took it apart. I didn't see it go in, I was busy trying to get the other one. He went into a climbing turn to starboard to try to get away. I locked up a Sidewinder and fired it. The missile followed him round the corner and went close over his port wing root. There was a bright orange flash close to the aircraft but it didn't blow up or anything.

Ward watched his wingman engage the two Daggers and saw the first one crash, then yet another of the enemy fighter-bombers came speeding past the nose of his aircraft. Estimating that the enemy plane was doing about 500kts (575mph) at 50ft, Ward racked his Sea Harrier into a tight turn to line up for snap attack and launched a Sidewinder. The missile rammed into the Dagger, blowing away part of the tail, and the aircraft dived into the ground, shedding pieces. Then, short of fuel and with only one missile between them, the two Sea Harriers headed back for their carrier.

On the available evidence, Thomas could claim the second machine he attacked only as 'possibly destroyed'. After the war, however, Argentine sources revealed that all three of the Daggers engaged with Sidewinders had been shot down. The three pilots reached the ground with relatively minor injuries—a remarkable testimony to the effectiveness of their ejection seats since all of them had been at ultra-low level when their aircraft were hit.

Also at this time, Lieutenant-Commander Alberto Philippi entered the south end of Falkland Sound, leading three Skyhawks of the 3rd Naval Fighter and Attack *Escuadrilla*. The new attack force sped up the waterway at low altitude, and the first ship they encountered was the already battered *Ardent*. The aircraft moved into line astern and wheeled into their bombing runs. Half a mile from his target, Philippi pulled up to 300ft, aligned his bomb sight on the warship and released his four 500lb, American-made 'Snakeye' bombs. These weapons were specially designed for release from low altitude, and as each left the aircraft four drag-plates opened at the tail to slow the bomb during its fall. The slower rate of fall would allow the aircraft to get clear before the weapons detonated, and would also give the bombs time to become 'live' before they hit the target.

From the bridge of his ship, Alan West watched the first salvo of bombs approach and disappear from view. Then there was a series of huge explosions. The captain was lifted off his feet and struck the deck head, then he fell in a heap on the deck. He got up in time to see the second of the Skyhawks, that piloted by Lieutenant Jose Arca, sweep low over the ship after releasing its bombs. *Ardent*'s machine-gunners maintained a steady fire at the plane, and West saw a row of holes appear across one of the wings. Immediately afterwards yet another bomb exploded against the ship's stern. The third Skyhawk to attack, piloted by Ensign Marcelo Marquez, failed to score any hits. After completing his attack, Philippi remained at low altitude and headed south-west down Falkland Sound, with the other Skyhawks following at two-mile intervals.

Passing over Goose Green at 10,000ft and heading for their patrol line, Lieutenant Clive Morell and Flight Lieutenant John Leeming of No 800 Squadron

---

DOUGLAS A-4P SKYHAWK

Role: Single-seat, carrier-based attack aircraft.

Power: One Wright J65 W-18 engine developing 8,500lb of thrust.

Armament: Two Mk 12 20mm cannon; up to 2,000lb of bombs.

Performance: Maximum speed (with warload, at low altitude) 575mph.

Normal operational take-off weight: 22,500lb

Dimensions: Span 27ft 6in; length 40ft 4in; wing area 260 sq ft.

Date of first production A-4B Skyhawk: Late 1956 (A-4P was the designation given to A-4Bs exported to Argentina).

heard a radio broadcast that *Ardent* was under attack. Looking down, Morell saw the bombs explode on the frigate:

> Having seen the bombs explode, I deduced that the attackers would probably exit going south-west down the Sound. I looked to where I thought they would be and they appeared, lo and behold, below a hole in the clouds.

The Sea Harriers dived at full throttle after the attackers, and Marquez, in the rear Skyhawk, was the first to sense danger. Later Philippi commented:

> A couple of minutes after attacking I thought we had escaped, when a shout from Marquez froze my heart: 'Harrier! Harrier!' I immediately ordered the tanks and bomb racks to be jettisoned in the hope we would be able to reach the safety of cloud ahead of us.

The Sea Harrier that Marquez had seen was Morell's, which was now gaining rapidly on Philippi's Skyhawk. The Royal Navy pilot launched a Sidewinder at the enemy fighter-bomber, and watched it home and explode close to its target. Philippi's first indication that he was being attacked was a powerful explosion at the rear of his aircraft, after which the nose pitched up violently. Unable to control the machine, Philippi ejected and came down in shallow water just off the coast. Clive Morell continued after the remaining Skyhawk in front of him—Arca's. His remaining Sidewinder refused to leave its launcher, so he satisfied himself with emptying his guns in the direction of the fighter-bomber. He saw no hits.

Speeding through the narrows at low altitude, Marquez appeared to be concentrating his attention on the fate of the two Skyhawks in front him. He did not notice John Leeming slide into position for a gun attack from behind on his aircraft. The RAF pilot recalled:

> He was at about zero feet, I was at zero plus 50. Still there was no sign that he had seen me; he was heading out as fast as he could. I fired a couple of tentative bursts, then my third splattered the sea around him. He must have realized what was happening then, because about a second later he rolled hard to starboard. But by then it was too late: I was within about 200 yards. Before he could start to pull round I put my sight on his cockpit, pressed the firing button and, as the first rounds struck, the aircraft exploded. I think the engine must have broken up because the aircraft just disintegrated.

Leeming pulled up sharply to avoid the rapidly growing cloud of debris in front of him, and, as he did so, Morell glanced back and saw the expanding fireball. His first horrified thought was that his wingman might have gone down, but Leeming reassured him with a brief radio call.

All of the events described, from the moment Steve Thomas first sighted the incoming Daggers until John Leeming swerved to avoid the debris from the Skyhawk, had taken place during the ten-minute period between 2.52 and 3.02 p.m.

By now *Ardent* was in dire distress, with a major fire blazing in her aft section. The frigate was taking on water rapidly and her steering gear was out of action.

With a heavy heart, Alan West gave the order to abandon ship and asked the frigate *Yarmouth* came alongside to take off survivors. West himself was the last to leave the ship. Twenty-two of the ship's crew had been killed and more than thirty injured.

None of the three Skyhawks involved in the final attack on *Ardent* survived the encounter. Clive Morell and John Leeming had each shot down one. Philippi ejected, but Marquez was killed. Jose Arca's Skyhawk suffered damage from the ship's return fire or from Morell's cannon shells, or perhaps both. Losing fuel from a punctured tank, Arca knew he could not return to the mainland, so he flew to Port Stanley and ejected.

After Philippi's attack, a second formation of three naval Skyhawks ran in to bomb ships in the landing area. These aircraft suffered no losses, but they also failed to score any hits with their bombs. That was the last attack of the day, and from then on the transports were allowed to continue their unloading operation unmolested.

Just over six hours after Alan West left her, the burning *Ardent* finally slid under the waves. With two unexploded bombs lodged in her hull, *Argonaut* was towed into San Carlos Water, where work began to defuse the weapons and remove them from the ship.

* * *

During the action on 21 May, the Argentine Navy and Air Force lost ten of the fifty or so Skyhawks and Daggers sent to attack the landing area—an unsustainable loss rate of 20 per cent; in addition, two Pucarás based on the Falklands were also shot down. Nine of these planes fell to attacks by Sea Harriers, one fell to a ground-launched Stinger missile, one was shot down by to a ship-launched missile and one was shot down by a Sea Harrier or small-arms fire from a ship, or both. The Sea Harriers suffered no losses.

The lack of proper air-to-air tactical training for the Argentine fighter-bomber pilots manifested itself throughout the action, and they had little awareness of how aircraft in an attack formation could provide mutual cover for each other using their cannon armament. When engaged by Sea Harriers, the Argentine fighter-bomber pilots never attempted to fight back or assist a comrade under attack.

By placing themselves in positions to draw the Argentine air attacks on themselves, the warships in the 'gun line' saved the vulnerable transport ships from a severe battering. The cost was not light: one frigate had been sunk and a frigate and a destroyer had been seriously damaged. Yet, despite this serious loss in material, the proximity of rescue ships and helicopters kept losses in personnel relatively low: 24 Royal Navy sailors were killed during the series of attacks that day.

The Argentine pilots had pressed home their low-altitude attacks with great bravery and determination. But, although they caused severe damage, they failed in their primary aim of defeating the amphibious landing operation. The unloading was allowed to proceed with little hinderance, and by the end of the day more than 3,000 British paratroops and commandos and nearly 1,000 tons of stores were ashore. Once the beach-head had been thus secured, the opportunity for the Argentine air units to have a decisive impact on the conflict had passed.

CHAPTER FIFTEEN

The Epic of 'Bravo November'

In the previous chapter, we observed that, while the possession of air superiority would not prevent a determined enemy from carrying out destructive air attacks, the raiding forces were themselves likely to suffer heavy losses. In this chapter, we again look at the Falklands conflict for an example of one type of operation, the free movement of troops and supplies by air, that becomes possible once a measure of air superiority has been secured. It also shows that a single medium-lift helicopter, resolutely handled, can exert an enormous influence on a small land campaign.

To SUPPORT the planned ground operations on the Falklands following the in-itial landings, No 18 Squadron of the RAF sent four Boeing Chinook medium-lift helicopters to the South Atlantic in the spring of 1982. The machines were transported as deck cargo on the container ship *Atlantic Conveyor*, together with a contingent of air and ground crewmen from the unit. Shortly before the landings, the container ship joined up with the British Task Force off the islands, and the Harriers and Sea Harriers she also brought south took off from her deck and flew to the aircraft carriers waiting to receive them.

Since they had not been intended to operate from ships, the RAF Chinooks were not fitted with folding rotor blades. Those loaded on to *Atlantic Conveyor* had their rotor blades removed so that they could be stowed more easily. On 25 May, in preparation for the fly-off scheduled for the following day, ground crew-men of No 18 Squadron began refitting the blades to the Chinooks.

Each blade was nearly 30ft long and weighed about 300lb, and there were three to be fitted each to the front and the rear rotor hubs, which were, respective-ly, 15ft and 18ft above the deck. A fork-lift truck was used to hoist each blade to the required height, the latter being suspended midway along its length from a rope attached to the lifting forks. Further ropes were tied to each end of the blade, their other ends held by men on deck, to guide it into position beside the hub. The men had no previous experience of fitting blades to big helicopters on the deck of a ship rolling in open sea and, in the words of Sergeant Steve Hitchman, it was 'a swine of a job'.

The problem was that, when the lifting truck's forks were raised or lowered, they moved in a series of jerks that caused the blades to flex along their length. The difficulty was further exacerbated by the movement of ship as she pitched and rolled. Hitchman continued: 'We had a man leaning over the rotor head as the blades were manoeuvred into position, ready to push the locking bolt into place. And a couple of times he nearly lost fingers.' During the afternoon of the 25th, the final blade was locked into place on the first of the Chinooks and, after completing engine running checks, Flying Officer John Kennedy took off for a brief air test. Thereafter the helicopter, radio call-sign 'Bravo November', would be used to transfer supplies between ships in the Task Force.

Soon after Kennedy had got airborne, the Task Force came under attack from a pair of Argentine Navy Super Etendard fighter-bombers, each of which launched an Exocet missile. The threat was detected in good time and the warships fired salvos of chaff rockets to seduce the Exocets clear of them. In this they were successful, but *Atlantic Conveyor* happened to be in the wrong place at the wrong time—behind a cloud of chaff that had drawn one of the missiles away. The Exocet emerged from the cloud of metallized strips, 're-acquired' the container ship and aligned itself on the new target. The weapon smashed into the ship's port quarter, where it detonated, starting several fires in the hold. Soon the fires were blazing out of control and *Atlantic Conveyor* was abandoned. Twelve men lost their lives in the incident, though everyone from No 18 Squadron escaped without injury.

The container ship foundered five days later with the charred remains of three Chinooks and several smaller helicopters on her deck. Only 'Bravo November' and one of the smaller helicopters had survived. The orphaned Chinook spent that night on the deck of the aircraft carrier *Hermes*, and the following day she flew to the San Carlos bridgehead.

At San Carlos, Squadron Leader Dick Langworthy took charge of the No 18 Squadron detachment, which comprised the Chinook, two four-man flight crews and nineteen technicians and supporting staff. The rest of the squadron personnel were put on one of the ships heading northwards out of the combat zone, for until the next batch of Chinooks reached the island there was no useful work for them to do.

All of the Chinook spare parts, special tools and servicing manuals intended for the detachment had been lost with *Atlantic Conveyor*, and there was speculation on how long the surviving helicopter could remain in an airworthy condition. 'Everybody thought we would be back on board ship in a couple of days,' recalled Chief Technician Tom Kinsella, in charge of the servicing team. 'The Chinook was bound to go unserviceable and that would be the end of our time ashore.'

BOEING CHINOOK HC Mk 1 (CH-47C)

Role: Medium-lift transport helicopter with a crew of four.

Power: Two Lycoming T55-L-11E turboshaft engines each developing 3,750shp.

Armament: None usually carried, though infantry nachine guns can be fired from open windows or from the open rear loading door.

Performance: Maximum speed 184mph; cruising cpeed 153mph.

Normal operational take-off weight: 46,000lb (maximum weight carried on operations about 27,000lb).

Dimensions: Rotor diameter 60ft; overall length (rotors turning) 99ft.

Date of first production CH-47C: February 1968.

For his part, Langworthy resolved to get as many flights as possible out of the Chinook before that happened. With a lifting capacity of 12 tons, it was the largest helicopter available to the British forces on the island; the Sea King, the next largest, could carry only 4 tons. Following the loss of so many helicopters on *Atlantic Conveyor*, the British land forces were desperately short of lifting capacity to sustain the advance on Port Stanley. For as long as she could be kept flying, 'Bravo November' would represent a significant proportion of that capacity.

As an initial task, 'Bravo November' was set to work transferring supplies from the transports moored in San Carlos Water to the storage areas ashore. Then, during the advance on Goose Green, she ferried artillery shells to the forward gun positions, carrying ten tons each time on a pallet slung below her fuselage. After the battle at Goose Green, she ferried Argentine prisoners, 60 at a time, to San Carlos. Describing these operations, Dick Langworthy commented:

> We threw away all the rules, operating the helicopter at its maximum all-up weight as often as we could. The aeroplane [*sic*] went on day after day with bits going unserviceable. But the engines kept going, the rotors kept turning and she continued to do the job.

After dark on 30 May, 'Bravo November' was sent deep into enemy-held territory, on a mission that was nearly her last. Reconnaissance patrols by the Special Air Service had discovered that the most of the Argentine troops had been withdrawn from Mount Kent, the strategically important strip of high ground ten miles west of Port Stanley. This was now a vacuum waiting to be filled, and three Royal Navy Sea Kings flew into the area and landed a detachment of commandos. Dick Langworthy followed in the Chinook, carrying 22 men and two 105mm guns in the fuselage and a further 105mm gun as an external load beneath the helicopter.

To enable them to navigate close to the ground in the darkness, the crew wore night-vision binoculars clipped to their flying helmets. Throughout much of the 45-mile flight, Langworthy kept the heavily laden Chinook at low altitude as he followed the series of ridge lines towards the objective. Occasionally a snow shower blotted out vision and forced him to climb well above the ground, but when the skies cleared he returned to low altitude.

The first problem arose when the Chinook reached the area where it was to put down the guns. Flight Lieutenant Tom Jones, the loadmaster responsible for the unloading operation, recalled:

> We had been led to believe that the ground on which we were to land would be relatively flat. Only when we arrived did we find it was on a sloping peat bog flanked on either side by stone rivers. We put down the underslung gun, no problem. Then we had to position the other two guns quite accurately in relation to the first. When Dick landed the Chinook, the back end sank into the peat so that we couldn't lower the ramp even with hydraulic pressure.

Langworthy eased the helicopter up a few feet, the ramp was lowered and he landed again. Now the exit was clear, and the gun crews toiled to move the first of the 2½-ton weapons to the opening and wheel it to the ground. They had not got far when a fire-fight broke out nearby between SAS men covering the operation and an Argentine patrol. Then, to add to the gunners' troubles, the red dim-lighting system in the rear of the helicopter failed. The cabin was plunged into darkness except for the shielded beams of hand torches, kept low to avoid drawing enemy fire. In case he needed to make a quick getaway, Langworthy kept the helicopter's engines running and the rotors turning.

Finally, the third and last of the guns was off-loaded, and the Chinook took off to return to Port San Carlos. The crew had no way of knowing it, but the worst was yet to come. The Chinook ran out at low altitude, giving the developing battle a wide berth, and almost immediately it ran into a thick snow shower. Blinded for a few all-important seconds, Langworthy allowed the helicopter to lose altitude and suddenly it shuddered as it struck something hard. Tom Jones, standing in the rear cabin, was thrown to the floor and had his flying helmet torn from his head. Inexplicably, at the time, the structure of the Chinook remained intact.

Only later would the crew learn that the helicopter had flopped down on the water in one of the small creeks to the west of Mount Kent. The wide, flat underside of the Chinook had skidded across the surface like a giant surf-board, throwing up a cloud of spray. Some of the water went into the air intakes and the two Lycoming engines began to lose power. As the engines ran down, there was a loss of hydraulic pressure, the power-assisted flying controls began to lose their effect and the helicopter became considerably heavier to handle. Thinking that a crash was imminent, the co-pilot released the escape door on his side of the cockpit. Dick Langworthy described what happened next:

> I shouted at the co-pilot to come on the controls with me. We both heaved on our collective pitch levers to increase the pitch of the running-down rotor blades, and that did the trick. The helicopter lifted just clear of the water, the spray ceased, and the engines started to wind up again.

With full power restored, Langworthy put the helicopter into a maximum-rate climb to get clear of high ground around him.

Soon afterwards the Chinook landed at San Carlos, and four very subdued men climbed out and made a grateful re-acquaintance with *terra firma*. Remarkably, apart from the loss of the co-pilot's door and minor damage to the rear loading ramp caused during the struggle to get the guns out, the helicopter had suffered little damage. 'After that incident we felt nothing was going to stop the Chinook keeping going for the rest of the war!' commented Tom Kinsella.

In the afternoon of 2 June, an operation by 'Bravo November' was to have far-reaching consequences for the campaign. The British ground-force commander had learned that Argentine troops had evacuated Fitzroy settlement some fifteen miles south-west of Port Stanley. He resolved to seize the area before the enemy commander changed his mind and perhaps re-occupied it.

At Goose Green, 'Bravo November' was 'hijacked' from her planned task and 81 paratroopers in full battle order clambered aboard her. The captain of the Chinook, Flight Lieutenant Dick Grose on this occasion, had only a vague idea of how much weight had been put aboard his helicopter. Standard assumptions regarding the weight of passengers plus their baggage were useless in this case: the battle-hardened troops expected to go into action soon after they landed, and each man carried as much ammunition as he could physically lift. Tom Jones described the conditions inside the helicopter:

> The paras were doing what we euphemistically call 'strap hanging'except that there were no straps to hang from. The seats were folded against the sides of the fuselage; the men were standing up and had to carry their weapons because there was no room to put them on the floor. The troops were packed in so tightly, they could hardly turn around. It was worse than a tube train in the rush hour.

The paratroops accepted their discomfort without complaint—they knew that the alternative to going by helicopter was a 30-mile forced march over difficult and broken country.

Fortunately for those on board, a vertical take-off in a helicopter is a fail-safe operation. If the machine is too heavy to get off the ground, it simply stays where it is. If it is light enough to get airborne, everything that follows works in its favour: as the machine gains forward speed its lifting capacity is increased, and as fuel is consumed the reserve of lifting capacity is increased further. Grose found that he could lift the heavily laden helicopter off the ground without difficulty, and he headed in the direction of Fitzroy. Throughout the flight the weather was poor, with low cloud covering the surrounding hills and visibility about two miles. Near Fitzroy the Chinook linked up with a couple of Army Scout helicopters, which led it to the landing area they had reconnoitred to the west of the settlement. The big helicopter landed, the ramp came down and within a quarter of a minute all the paratroops were outside and flat on their stomachs, weapons levelled ready to return fire. The move had passed unnoticed by the enemy, however, and the men began moving out to establish a defensive perimeter.

Grose returned to Goose Green, collected a further 75 paratroops and flew those to Fitzroy. It had been a bold operation and one that involved a degree of risk—there had been no time to reconnoitre the helicopter's route, and if it had flown over an Argentine position and been shot down there might have been heavy loss of life. It was a gamble, the sort that must sometimes be taken if there is a likelihood of shortening a conflict and preventing even greater losses.

During the days that followed, 'Bravo November' resumed her normal transport duties, flying over friendly territory. As British forces advanced on Port Stanley, the Chinook joined the shuttle service moving artillery shells from Teal Inlet to the gun positions around Mount Kent which were bombarding the Argentine positions. The 30-mile round trip took about 45 minutes, and the Chinook flew up to fifteen such missions each day, her two crews flying on alternate days.

On 7 June there was a break in the routine, when 'Bravo November' was sent to pick up two Navy Sea King helicopters that had suffered damage. Carrying one Sea King at a time as an underslung load, the Chinook transported the helicopters to their operating base near Port San Carlos. And on 8 June 'Bravo November' transported 64 wounded men in a single lift from Fitzroy to the hospital ship *Uganda* lying off the coast.

Of the underslung loads transported by 'Bravo November', the pilots found the pallets of artillery ammunition the easiest to carry: the load was immensely heavy but relatively small, and in flight it was stable in the airflow. Loads that were less dense sometimes developed a will of their own in flight, and were much more difficult to handle. On 14 June Dick Grose was called upon to fly an 8-ton steel girder bridge from Fitzroy, where it had been assembled by Army engineers, to Murrell. Flying Officer Colin Miller, co-pilot on the flight, explained the problems caused by this particular load:

> The girder bridge was quite heavy but it was very flat, and once we started moving with it under the Chinook it generated its own lift. Almost immediately it became unstable, swinging from side to side on its loading chains. We had to slow down to 20 knots to let it stabilize—though at no point was it fully stable—[and] from then on fly the helicopter very slowly and very carefully. That bridge was a bloody awful load!

As the Chinook was in the process of manoeuvring the bridge into position, assisted by Army engineers on the ground, the word came through that the Argentine forces on the islands had surrendered.

* * *

The story of 'Bravo November' on the Falklands is a text-book example of how a single aircraft of the right type, in the right place and at the right time, can have considerable influence on the course of a conflict. Now, more than a decade afterwards, that particular Chinook is still in service. One might have expected that she would have pride of place in a military museum, or be sitting as gate guardian at an RAF station to inspire future generations of helicopter crews. In fact, at the time of writing she is at the Boeing Helicopter plant in Philadelphia, undergoing a year-long modification programme to bring her to the latest CH-47D standard. When the work is completed, in the summer of 1993, she is due to return to the United Kingdom to resume her place in a front-line squadron.

CHAPTER SIXTEEN

Precision Attack—By Night

When Iraqi forces invaded Kuwait in August 1990 and sparked off the crisis in the Persian Gulf, the US Air Force's 48th Tactical Fighter Wing was equipped with the General Dynamics F-111F 'Aardvark' swing-wing attack plane. The unit was based at Lakenheath in England and its primary role was that of night attack using precision-guided munitions. This account chronicles the activities of the Wing during the conflict and describes ways in which it exploited the capabilities of its unique equipment.

THE DEVELOPMENT of air-launched guided weapons that are effective against pin-point land targets has been long and arduous. Since 1944 several such weapons have been introduced into service, but most of them failed to live up to their maker's expectations when they were used in combat. Only in the 1970s, with the advent of the laser-guided bomb (LGB), did a weapon exist that could really achieve the accuracy necessary to destroy such targets under combat conditions. Since the mid-1980s, the 48th Tactical Fighter Wing has been equipped with two basic types of precision-guided munition, the LGB and the more accurate (but also more expensive) electro-optically guided bomb (EOGB).

* * *

By 1990 the General Dynamics F-111 was what is euphemistically called 'a mature design'—or, in the words of one of the pilots of the 48th TFW, most of the unit's planes were 'old enough to vote'. The 48th was the only unit to be equipped with the F model of the famous aircraft, the final production version which was optimized for the night attack role with precision-guided weapons.

The F model carried a Pave Tack pod under the fuselage, to enable it to laser-designate targets for its LGBs; alternatively, the aircraft could carry a data-link pod for the control of EOGBs in flight. During attacks with these weapons, the plane's WSO (weapon systems officer) observed the target during the final part of the bomb's trajectory on a TV-type screen in the cockpit of the aircraft. These video pictures were taped for later analysis, and every reader will have seen the spectacular video footage of attacks with LGBs and EOGBs during the Gulf War. As well as the two main types of precision-guided munition, the F-111 could carry almost any unguided weapon on the US Air Force inventory.

* * *

In August 1990 the US President, George Bush, ordered his armed forces to implement Operation 'Desert Shield', initially with the aim of preventing Iraqi forces from advancing into Saudi Arabia. As part of this move, Colonel Tom Lennon, commander of the 48th TFW, received instructions to deploy part of his force into the crisis area. On the 25th, eighteen F-111Fs took off from Lakenheath and, supported by KC-135 tankers, flew non-stop to the Royal Saudi Air Force base at Taif near Mecca. At the time there were no precision-guided munitions in the new theatre, so each F-111F carried four LGBs or four EOGBs to produce an initial stock of these weapons at the new base. Within 48 hours of the arrival of the first aircraft at Taif, the unit had fully armed planes on ground alert there.

From the start, it was accepted that, if hostilities commenced, the 48th TFW would fly almost all (perhaps all) of its missions by night. Thus assured, the commander ordered his crews to begin an intensive programme of training flights to familiarize themselves with night operations over the desert. Tom Lennon recalled:

> Having so long to prepare for combat was great. It allowed us to practise operations with very large packages of aircraft. It allowed us to convince the Saudis that we needed to do business differently on their airfields, with mass night comms-out [radio-silent] launches, mass rejoins on the tankers, things that we don't practise in peace time.

The unit was also able to practise night, low-level operations over the desert, with aircraft flying on the terrain-following radar (TFR), initially at 400ft and later going down to 200ft. The F-111s also practised the difficult and demanding flight profiles necessary to deliver precision-guided munitions from low altitude.

The United Nations Security Council's deadline for the withdrawal of Iraqi troops from Kuwait expired at midnight on 15 January 1991. In the afternoon of the 16th, Coalition operational units received orders to execute Operation 'Desert Storm', the attack on Iraqi forces, during the early hours of the following morning.

The initial wave of air strikes hit numerous targets in Iraq and Kuwait. Tom Lennon explained how his force was used:

> It was a maximum effort: we launched 54 F-111Fs out of 64 and 53 of them went into action that night. If I had had 60 planes available, I would have sent all 60.

The aircraft were split into forces of four to six planes and delivered attacks on the chemical weapons storage bunkers at H-3, Salman Pak and Ad Diwaniyah, and on the airfields at Balad and Jalibah in Iraq and Ali Al Salem and Al Jaber in Kuwait. The attacking F-111Fs received fighter and SAM-suppression support at their target areas, but they were on their own while en route to and from their targets. Planes making for the same target flew singly at low altitude in trail, with a spacing of about a minute (about 8½ miles) between each.

Tom Lennon led the deepest penetration by the Wing that night, a six-plane strike on Balad airfield north of Baghdad. The commander and his wing aircraft hit designated buildings in the airfield's maintenance complex with EOGBs, then the remaining F-111Fs laid area-denial mines across the ends of each of the runways and among the hardened aircraft shelters (HASs). The aim of the attack was

---

GENERAL DYNAMICS F-111F

Role: Two-seat, swing-wing, night precision-attack aircraft.

Power: Two Pratt & Whitney TF30-P-100 turbofan engines each rated at 25,100lb of thrust with afterburner.

Armament: On normal operations a bomb load of up to 8,000lb was carried. Typical loads were four 2,000lb LGBs, or four 500lb LGBs, or four 2,000lb EOGBs (in this configuration the aircraft carried a data-transmission pod under the fuselage, to receive video pictures transmitted from the weapons after release and transmit guidance signals to them).

Performance: Maximum speed (clean, at 35,000ft) 1,450mph (Mach 2.2), (clean, at low altitude) 800mph (Mach 1.2)

Maximum gross take-off weight: 100,000lb.

Dimensions: Span (wings fully forward) 63ft, (wings fully swept) 31ft 11½in; length 77ft; wing area (wings fully forward) 525 sq ft.

Date of first production F-111F: August 1971.

---

to neutralize this important airfield during the critical few hours that followed, by making the movement of Iraqi aircraft on the ground hazardous until the mines could be cleared. In that it was successful.

During the period leading up to the conflict, commanders of air attack units had been told to expect 'worst-case' losses of around 10 per cent of sorties flown during the initial air strikes. On that basis Tom Lennon feared he might lose six planes during his unit's initial wave of attacks. In the event, all the F-111Fs returned safely; two had damage from small-arms fire, but in each case it was minor and repaired easily.

During the second night of the war, the 17th/18th, the unit dispatched 35 F-111s to hit several more targets in Iraq. Four planes carrying EOGBs headed for Saddam Hussein's summer palace at Tikrit, which housed one of the dictator's command centres. On the way to the objective, a MiG-29 'Fulcrum' attempted to engage the raiders, starting an intercept on each one in turn. The Iraqi pilot nibbled down the line and finally slid behind the last F-111 in the trail. His intended victim then folded back its wings and accelerated to maximum speed at low altitude, and the high-speed chase continued for more than 70 miles before the MiG gave up the struggle. In the meantime, the three remaining F-111Fs reached Tikrit and delivered their EOGBs with great precision. The palace was devastated.

Also that night, a six-plane striking force carried out an experimental attack on HASs at Mudaysis airfield. This attack was to have far-reaching consequences. Mudaysis lay outside the main Iraqi SAM-defended area, so the raiders could attack in safety from medium altitude. The F-111Fs released their LGBs from altitudes around 20,000ft and each swing-wing bomber carried out four separate runs, aiming a single 2,000lb weapon at an individual HAS on each run. The aircraft flew in trail, following each other around the same oblong 'race-track' pattern. After guiding its first bomb to impact, the leading F-111F turned and flew round the 'race-track', then turned and made its second bomb run flying the same track as for the first. The F-111Fs repeated the process for as long as they had ordnance remaining. That night the raiders scored hits on 23 hardened shelters, and those that contained planes produced spectacular secondary explosions when they were hit.

The Iraqi air plan, such as it was, depended on the hardened shelters to keep combat planes safe until they were required to go into action against Coalition ground forces. Undoubtedly the ease with which the F-111Fs destroyed the HASs and their contents at Mudaysis came as a nasty shock to the Iraqi High Command, and this played a part in prompting the later decision to fly the most modern combat planes out of the country.

During the initial attacks, the Wing dispatched several small striking forces each night, aiming to cause damage at as wide a spread of targets as possible. After a few days the tactics changed, with far larger forces of aircraft being sent against far fewer targets. As Tom Lennon explained:

> After the first night we didn't do anything with six aircraft. When we went after something, we would go after it big time. We would put 20 to 24 airplanes on one airfield at one time. If we had to hit a target, we hit it with everything we had, all at once, and got out of there.

During the night of 20/21 January, the Wing sent twenty F-111Fs to deliver a set-piece attack on Balad airfield. By then the threat from Iraqi fighters and long-range SAMs was judged to have been contained, and even when passing over the most heavily defended areas the F-111Fs could fly at medium level. These aircraft now attacked from altitudes of between 12,000 and 20,000ft, where they were beyond reach of most of the anti-aircraft artillery (AAA) fire. In a repeat of the tactics used over Mudaysis, the F-111Fs cruised over the enemy airfield, guiding individual 2,000lb LGBs at the strategic points on the runways and taxiways. When released from medium altitude, the LGB proved particularly effective for this purpose: the weapon impacted at a steep angle and penetrated the concrete surface before it detonated to produce a large crater.

Despite the constant harassment at the hands of their American counterparts whenever they got airborne, there were still Iraqi fighter pilots willing to make determined attempts to engage the raiders. As the last F-111F was leaving Balad that night, a MiG-29 closed in to attack it and locked on its radar. Captain Jerry

---

OPERATION OF PAVE TACK ATTACK POD

When the F-111F reached the area of the target, its Weapon Systems Officer (WSO) operated a small hand controller to steer the Pave Tack head until it was pointing at the target. The head was linked to an infra-red TV camera, whose picture was displayed on a screen in the cockpit. The target was placed under the aiming reticle in the centre of the screen, a process which aligned the laser head on the target. The laser beam was then turned on, the laser-guided bomb or bombs were released and the weapons homed on the laser energy reflected from the target.

Hanna, the WSO in the bomber, recalled that from then on everything happened very quickly indeed:

> We immediately initiated a high-speed combat descent, the pilot got the wings back and we went screaming down hill. Puking chaff, we went from 19,000 to about 4,000 feet in a heartbeat! The adrenalin was really pumping, Jim [the pilot] was busy trying get the plane close to the ground, I was on radio hollering at the AWACS that we had been jumped by a MiG and to get the F-18s coming back in our direction.

Hanna set up the terrain-following radar so that it would take automatic control of the plane as soon as the latter got close to the ground. By following the contours closely at maximum speed, the F-111F made a very difficult target. Before that happened, however, the MiG suddenly broke away. No doubt aware that American fighters were converging on him, the Iraqi pilot probably thought he had done all that honour required.

The large-scale attacks from medium altitude became the main mode of operation by the F-111Fs, and their tactics were continually refined. During attacks on clusters of weapons storage bunkers or HASs, the bombers used the so-called 'Wagon Wheel' tactic, with a number of race-track flight patterns arranged like the spokes of a wheel centred on the target. Lieutenant Bradley Seipel, a WSO on the unit, described what it was like to be part of a multi-aircraft attack of this type on the HASs dotted around an enemy airfield:

> It was awesome. After you released your bomb [from medium altitude] it was in the air for nearly a minute. While you marked your own target with the laser, on the Pave Tack video screen you saw this shelter blow up, then you saw that shelter blow up, then you saw another one blow up. Then the one that you had your laser on blew up.

Using such methods, the Wing fought its own battle to dismember the Iraqi Air Force. And because it could deliver the precision weapons at night, it did so with minimal risk to its aircraft and crews.

Lieutenant-Colonel Tommy Crawford, the Wing's Assistant Deputy Commander for Operations, described the Iraqi SAM and AAA defences at this stage of the war. In his view, against high-flying night raiders, they were ineffective:

> They fired lots of SAMs. At first there were cases of the guys on the ground holding the radar lock-on throughout an engagement. But with the HARM firers [Wild Weasel aircraft firing High Speed Anti-Radiation Missiles at the radars] supporting us they didn't survive long if they did that. Then the SAM batteries changed their tactics. The radar would come on, they would lock on and fire their missile, then shut down the radar. They would send the missile up ballistically and hope that we didn't turn or anything. We could see them coming, so it was pretty easy to avoid them.

Almost all of the AAA was unaimed barrage fire, which could be ignored at altitudes above 15,000ft.

As well as carrying out attacks on airfields, the Wing also struck at munitions production and storage facilities. One of these targets that came in for particular attention was the huge Latifiyah munitions production complex and research centre near Baghdad. The Wing mounted four separate attacks against this target, each with between 20 to 24 aircraft.

On 25 January Iraqi Army engineers opened valves to discharge millions of gallons of crude oil into the waters of the Persian Gulf, producing a huge slick off the coast. The move was intended to make it more difficult for Coalition forces to launch an amphibious landing operation in the area, and it is questionable whether it could have been effective (even if such an operation had been planned). But what is certain is that the act caused a great deal of pollution and posed a severe threat to marine wildlife in the area. President Bush termed it an act of 'environmental terrorism' and asked his military commanders to examine ways of bringing it to a halt. The 48th Wing was given the task of destroying the two pumping stations at Al Ahmadi in Kuwait that were pushing the oil into the sea. Both targets lay close to areas of civilian housing, so an extremely precise attack was required.

The operation against the pumping stations took place during the night of 26/27 January and, because of its political importance, the attackers employed a large measure of 'overkill'. Five F-111Fs (including two reserve aircraft) took off for the mission, each carrying two 2,000lb EOGBs and a data-link pod. One F-111F suffered a technical malfunction and was unable to take part, but the rest of the mission went off without a hitch. Flying supersonic at 20,000ft, one of the planes lobbed an EOGB towards the first pumping station from more than 20 miles away. The plane then entered a sharp diving turn and sped out of the area. A second F-111F, flying parallel to the coast on a north-westerly heading more than 50 miles out to sea and beyond the reach of the defences, then took control of the bomb and guided it throughout the rest of its flight. Bradley Seipel, WSO in the controlling plane, observed the video picture transmitted from the camera in the nose of the missile and steered the weapon in for a direct hit on the first pumping station.

Captain Michael Russell, Seipel's pilot, then turned his aircraft through 180 degrees and the flew south-east, parallel to the coast, as a second F-111F lobbed an EOGB in the direction of the second pumping station. Again Seipel took con-

---

OPERATION OF ELECTRO-OPTICAL GUIDED BOMB (EOGB)

When it operated with this weapon, the F-111F had a special data-link pod mounted under the rear fuselage. The EOGB was aimed and released in the same way as a normal free-fall bomb, and was controlled only during the final part of its trajectory. The weapon was fitted with a TV-type camera in the nose, whose picture was relayed by radio link to the controlling aircraft (which might or might not be the one that released the weapon). The picture seen from the nose of the bomb was viewed in the cockpit of the controlling aircraft on a screen in front of the WSO, and the latter operated a hand controller to send steering signals to correct the missile's flight path during the final fifteen seconds or so to impact.

---

[146]

trol of the EOGB in flight and guided the weapon to score a direct hit. The entire attack, from the release of the first bomb to the impact of the second, took about five minutes. Then the five F-111Fs, between them bearing eight unused EOGBs, returned to Taif. The video footage transmitted to the aircraft from the cameras in the missiles later featured in news broadcasts shown all over the world. With both of the offending pumping stations wrecked, the flow of oil into the sea ceased.

On 26 January the Wing's earlier campaign against HASs brought a sudden and quite unexpected bonus for the Coalition as Iraqi combat planes started to flee to neutral Iran. The move continued for several days and more than a hundred Iraqi aircraft made the one-way flight. None of the planes were returned, and since then several have been incorporated into the Iranian Air Force.

During the night of 29/30 January the Wing shifted its attention to the bridges along the Iraqi supply routes into Kuwait. The first such attack was on bridges over the Hawr Al Hammar Lake north-west of Basrah, and in the days that followed the unit mounted a systematic campaign against bridges over the Tigris and Euphrates rivers. Modern steel and concrete bridges are difficult targets for air attack, however, as Lieutenant Dave Giachetti explained:

> With precision-guided munitions, hitting the bridge was not a problem. The problem was hitting it at a weak part, a point where the weapon would cause structural damage and drop a span. If you didn't hit it exactly on the abutment at either end, or where the supports were, the bomb would often go through the pavement, leaving a neat round hole that they could easily repair.

One of the most difficult such targets proved to be the twin highway bridges over the River Tigris near Basrah, which required three separate attacks before they were put out of action.

After a period of trial and error, the Wing evolved the optimum tactics for use against the different types of bridge. One method that proved particularly effective was to have two planes each aiming four 2,000lb EOGBs at the middle support sections of the bridge and two planes each aiming four 2,000lb LGBs at the abutments at each end. During these attacks the aircraft flew race-track patterns and each bomb was guided individually to the required impact point. Where an important bridge had been rendered unusable, Iraqi Army engineers would often erect a pontoon bridge alongside it to keep the traffic moving. These flimsy structures proved easy targets for LGBs, however, and a single hit at either end would shatter the structure, releasing the remaining pontoons to float downstream.

Early in February the Wing was asked to join in the general attack on Iraqi tanks and armoured vehicles in the battle zone, as part of the final preparations for the Coalition ground offensive. Individual vehicles lay in bulldozed scrapes 10ft deep and were covered with sandbags to give added protection. Each vehicle was thus a small pin-point target that was largely invulnerable to air attack unless the latter came from almost vertically above. The Iraqis had no inkling of the effectiveness of the F-111F and its Pave Tack equipment, however. Planes traversing the area on their way to and from other targets brought back infra-red video film of the dug-in vehicles. It was found that the bulldozer scrapes produced a distinctive infra-red signature which showed up clearly on Pave Tack.

Staff officers at the Wing devised a plan to use LGBs against the enemy vehicles, dropped from F-111Fs flying at medium altitude so that the bombs would impact at a steep angle to achieve maximum destructive effect. Each aircraft was to carry four 500lb LGBs and release one at a time and guide it to impact on an individual vehicle, then repeat the process.

During the night of 5/6 February the Wing mounted an operational trial to test out the new tactics. Tom Lennon and Tommy Crawford each took off in an F-111F and attacked a Republican Guard unit deployed in the desert, and the eight LGBs they carried scored hits on seven enemy vehicles. These tactics did not appear in any military text-book, and Crawford later quipped that if he had stood up at Staff College a year earlier and proposed using the F-111F in this way he would have probably been laughed out of the room!

Laughter or not, the tactics proved highly productive. The F-111Fs achieved their greatest success during the night of 13/14 February, when 46 aircraft attacked the dug-in vehicles. The planes were credited with scoring hits on no fewer than 132 tanks and armoured vehicles. Initially there were doubts regarding the ability of the small LGBs to knock out tanks, but this ability was confirmed to the full when Coalition ground troops later occupied the area.

On 27/28 February, the last night of the conflict, two F-111Fs attacked a military command centre buried deep underground at Al Taji near Baghdad. Each plane aircraft carried a 4,700lb 'Bunker-Buster' LGB, a deep-penetration weapon that had been hastily produced specifically for use in attacks on such targets. One of the new bombs hit the bunker and caused a small puff of smoke to blow out of an entrance to the structure. Then, a few seconds later, came a large secondary explosion that was thought to have destroyed the interior of the bunker.

* * *

During the conflict in the Gulf, the 48th Tactical Fighter Wing inflicted severe damage on several airfields and munitions production and storage facilities. The F-111Fs destroyed a dozen permanent bridges and caused severe damage to 52 more, and they hit 920 Iraqi tanks and armoured vehicles (one-seventh of all of those destroyed by Coalition forces) and 245 hardened aircraft shelters (two-thirds of the total destroyed). Moreover, in achieving these impressive results, the Wing did not not lose a single aircraft in combat.

CHAPTER SEVENTEEN

St Valentine's Day Shoot-Down

During its attacks on targets in Iraq, the Royal Air Force lost six Tornado fighter-bombers in combat. The last fell on the morning of 14 February 1991 during an attack on Al Taqaddum airfield near Baghdad, shot down by a couple of SA-3 missiles. This is the story behind that loss.

IT WAS GETTING LIGHT at Muharraq airfield, Bahrain, as Wing Commander John Broadbent took off at the head of a raiding force comprising eight Tornados and four Buccaneers. Each Tornado carried two 1,000lb laser-guided bombs (LGBs) and each Buccaneer carried a Pave Spike designator pod to laser-mark the targets for the Tornados' bombs. The crews were briefed to carry out yet another attack on the hardened aircraft shelters (HASs) at the important Al Taqaddum airfield near Baghdad.

The attack was planned to commence at 8.40 a.m. and it was to take place in broad daylight (unlike the Pave Tack day/night attack system fitted to the F-111Fs described in the previous chapter, the less-advanced Pave Spike equipment carried by the Buccaneers was a daylight-only system). Taking off at about the same time as the RAF planes were those of the US Air Force defence-suppression package to support the attack—two F-15C Eagle air superiority fighters, two F-4G Wild Weasel aircraft carrying radar-homing missiles and two EF-111 Raven radar-jamming aircraft.

The Tornados and Buccaneers arrived over the target at the briefed attack altitudes, around 20,000ft, and the crews found the skies clear of cloud, though there was some haze lower down. Al Taqaddum had been one of the most heavily defended airfields in Iraq, but by this stage of the war the SAM sites in the area had taken a severe battering and they had been inactive during the recent attacks.

The main raiding force flew in elements of three aircraft, each of which comprised a pair of Tornados and an attendant Buccaneer. After releasing its bombs, each Tornado turned away and headed out of the defended area, while the navigator in the Buccaneer laser-marked the selected HAS until the bombs impacted. A couple of 1,000-pounders striking the roof of a HAS within a few feet of each other and a fraction of a second apart would punch a sizeable hole through the structure, wrecking anything inside.

At the controls of one of the last Tornados to attack, Flight Lieutenant Rupert Clark commenced his bombing run. The attack was progressing more or less normally until he was five seconds short of the bomb-release point, when he noticed a brief burst of signals from an enemy missile control radar on the plane's radar homing and warning receiver (RHWR). Clark opted to continue with the attack, and there was no further indication from the enemy radar until he reached the release point. One bomb left the aircraft cleanly, but from then on things quickly turned sour.

The second LGB remained stubbornly on its rack, defying all efforts by the navigator, Flight Lieutenant Steven Hicks, to get it to release. Shortly after that came a panic radio call that raised the hairs on the back of Clark's neck: 'Double missile launch over the target!' Now the Tornado's RHWR showed clear indications that missile command guidance signals were being beamed in its direction: a missile had been launched and was being guided on to the aircraft! Hicks called 'Break left!' and began releasing chaff. Clark selected full power, lowered the plane's manoeuvring flaps and threw the aircraft into a tight turn. Later he recalled:

> We were going through north when there was this huge explosion and I felt the blast wave hit the aircraft. It was obvious what had happened. I shouted to Steve 'You OK?', but there was no reply.

The missile was a Soviet-built SA-3 'Goa' and it had detonated a few feet from the bomber's port side. Scores of high-velocity fragments tore into the plane, causing widespread damage. With a rush of air, the cabin depressurized itself through a 2in diameter hole that suddenly appeared in the left side of the canopy just in front of Clark's head. As the pilot looked around the cockpit to assess the situation, he realized how lucky he had been to escape serious injury. On the warning panel there were too many red lights for him to count. The reflector glass of the head-up display had disappeared altogether. The instrument panel was a shambles with only two dials seemingly intact, but the instruments, hydraulic gauges, both read zero.

Clark had no time to dwell on this catalogue of problems, however, for he had a more immediate threat to deal with. Almost certainly there was a second missile coming his way:

> I moved the stick, overbanked the aircraft, and pulled back. Then I saw the second missile coming at me. It was coming up vertically, waggling as it guided on to me. I pulled on the stick as hard as I could, there was nothing else I could do. The missile disappeared from view going behind and to the right of the aircraft. There was another explosion as it went off.

Again Clark shouted to ask how his navigator was, and again there was no reply. Normally he could look round and see Hicks's smiling face. He now looked over each shoulder and, seeing nothing of his friend, began to fear the worst.

Clark found that he was bleeding from several cuts, though none appeared to be serious. Like Randy Cunningham and Willie Driscoll over Vietnam (see Chapter 13), his immediate concern was to put as much distance as possible between himself and the target. He had no wish to be taken prisoner, and he knew that for every minute he held the aircraft in the air he and his crewman would be six or seven miles closer to possible rescue.

A brief scan around the exterior of the Tornado revealed considerable damage. The wings and the external fuel tanks were peppered with holes and, looking

---

PANAVIA TORNADO GR Mk 1

Role: Two-seat, swing-wing attack and reconnaissance aircraft.

Power: Two Turbo-Union RB199 turbofan engines each rated at 15,000lb of thrust with afterburners.

Armament: Maximum load carried on operations comprised two JP233 airfield-denial weapons containers weighing a total of 10,300lb or up to eight 1,000lb bombs (during attacks with laser-guided bombs the aircraft carried two or three 1,000lb LGBs); two Mauser 27mm cannon; two AIM-9L Sidewinder infra-red homing missiles for self-defence.

Performance: Maximum speed (with full warload, at low altitude) 680mph, (clean, at altitude) over 1,450mph (Mach 2.2).

Maximum gross take-off weight: 60,000lb.

Dimensions: Span (wings fully forward) 45ft 7in, (wings fully swept) 28ft 2in; lerngth 54ft 9½in; wing area (wings fully forward) 323 sq ft.

Date of first production Tornado GR.1: June 1979.

---

back, he could see fuel streaming out and leaving a long white trail behind the aircraft. On the starboard wing, one of the slats had been blasted away from the leading edge and was sticking above the wing like some obscene gesture.

With the hydraulic system wrecked, the Tornado had automatically reverted to the manual flying mode. Clark found that if he pushed hard on the stick the plane would slowly respond. He had no way of telling if either of the engines was working, though from the way the plane handled it was obvious that they were producing little if any thrust. Ever the optimist, Clark went through the emergency procedure to restart the engines after a double flame-out. It made no difference.

A Tornado with no flying instruments makes a lousy glider. Clark raised the plane's nose a couple of times in an attempt to extend its glide, but each time he did so the noise level—and with it the speed—dropped. He had no idea which noise level equated to the stalling speed of the Tornado in that condition, and he had no wish to stall the plane to find out. He lowered the nose until the wind noise sounded about right, and accepted the resultant rate of descent.

As the plane descended below what he judged to be 10,000ft, Clark found the Tornado progressively more difficult to control. He had to apply more and more right stick to hold the wings horizontal, until in the end the stick was almost fully to the right—and still the aircraft wanted to 'lean' to the left. There was no point on hanging on any longer: he wanted to abandon the aircraft before he lost control entirely.

He tried one more time to call his navigator, and when there was still no answer he let go of the stick, placed both hands on the firing handle between his legs and yanked hard. In the Tornado, the ejection seats are interconnected so that, if the pilot pulls his handle, the navigator's seat is fired first and the pilot's seat follows shortly afterwards. Clark heard a loud bang and the cockpit filled with swirling black smoke as the rockets fired to lift off the canopy. Then came another loud bang in the rear cockpit, as the navigator's seat fired. Then it was Clark's turn:

I got the kick up the backside as my seat fired. I heard or sensed each action in turn: the cartridges firing in my seat, my drogue gun going, and my seat tumbling as I left the aircraft. I was fully conscious and I remember thinking, when are all these explosions going to stop? Then suddenly there was dead silence, absolutely no noise at all, and I was hanging from my parachute.

After the traumatic events of the previous few minutes—of being hit by the missiles, of trying to keep the plane airborne, of ejecting—that silence was like a sudden and unexpected gift from the gods.

Clark glanced down to observe the final moments of his crippled aircraft. It continued down in a sweeping turn to the left until it plunged into the ground with a hollow-sounding *boomphf*. The wreckage immediately burst into flames, fed by the remaining fuel in the tanks. A cloud of dense black smoke rose quickly to mark the impact point. Next came a succession of loud crackles and bangs as 27mm cannon shells in the plane's ammunition magazines 'cooked off' in the heat. Meanwhile Clark was assessing his direction of drift, trying to gauge where his parachute would deposit him. The predicted landing point looked disconcertingly close to the pile of wreckage now blazing fiercely on the ground. The pilot needed no reminding that, as well as the cannon shells, somewhere in the twisted remains of the aircraft lay a 1,000lb bomb and a couple of Sidewinder missiles. He hauled hard on the rigging lines to steer himself away from the danger. Shortly before Clark touched down, he saw his navigator's parachute land some distance away. The canopy deflated and there was no sign of life, and it seems certain that Steve Hicks never regained consciousness after the detonation of the first missile.

The pilot made a good landing a couple of hundred yards from the funeral pyre of his plane. He released his parachute harness, then his combat survival training took over and he cast an eye over the landscape for somewhere to hide while the rescue operation was set in train. Yet the flat desert landscape extended for more than a thousand yards in every direction. Clark recalled:

You could have put a cricket pitch almost anywhere there and you wouldn't have needed to use the heavy roller. There was nothing at all to hide behind. Just off to the south were what looked like some big sandstone blocks, [and] I thought that was the best place to head. So I picked up the survival pack and started legging it in that direction. The pack was heavy and after about 200 metres I decided to get rid of the dinghy. I started to open the pack, very carefully so as not to inflate the dinghy, when *psssssss* . . . the bright orange dinghy started to inflate itself!

He dropped the dinghy and continued his long jog in the direction of the outcrop, though in retrospect it is clear that the Iraqis would have had to be deaf and blind not to have noticed his arrival. The wreckage of the Tornado was marked with a pillar of thick black smoke hundreds of feet high, with a series of bangs to draw attention to it. Nearby lay the pilot's discarded parachute. From there a trail of footprints lead to the bright orange dinghy sitting incongruously on the desert floor, and from there a further line of footprints led to the British airman heading away from the scene as fast as his legs could carry him.

Rupert Clark's period of freedom lasted less than a quarter of an hour, before a civilian on a motor cycle and brandishing a rifle came speeding across the desert towards him. Seeing that he had no chance of escape, Clark raised his hands in surrender, to begin a short but extremely unpleasant spell as a 'guest' of the Iraqi Government.

Finale

THE PURPOSE of this narrative has been to provide the reader with 'a feel' for the true nature of aerial warfare in its many and varied forms. The changes that have occurred in military aviation during the eight decades since its inception have indeed been far-reaching. Even in areas where aviation was not itself the driving force in pushing forward the limits of technology, it has never lagged far behind the limits of what was possible. Yet, although we have observed enormous transformations in this area of human endeavour, one set of values has remained almost constant throughout—the bravery, the determination and the resourcefulness of those who have made the sky their chosen arena for battle.

Glossary

AAA	Anti-aircraft artillery.
AI	Airborne interception (radar).
ASV	Air-to-surface vessel (radar).
EOGB	Electro-optically guided bomb.
Flensburg	German homing device to pick up signals from 'Monica' radar.
GCI	Ground controlled interception (radar).
Geschwader	World War II *Luftwaffe* flying unit with an established strength of about 96 aircraft.
Gruppe	*Luftwaffe* flying unit with an established strength of about 30 aircraft.
HAS	Hardened aircraft shelter.
hp	Horsepower.
H2S	Microwave ground-mapping radar fitted to RAF bombers.
LGB	Laser-guided bomb.
Metox	German warning receiver fitted to U-boats, to pick up transmissions from early versions of ASV radar.
'Monica'	Tail-warning radar fitted to RAF bombers.
Naxos	German receiver and homing device to pick up signals from enemy microwave radars, carried by night fighters and naval vessels, including U-boats.
nm	Nautical miles.
PR	Photographic reconnaissance.
RHWR	Radar homing and warning receiver.
SAM	Surface-to-air missile.
shp	Shaft horsepower.
Sidewinder	US-designed air-to-air, infra-red homing guided missile.
Sparrow	US-designed air-to-air, semi-active radar homing guided missile.
TFR	Terrain-following radar.
WSO	Weapon systems officer (crewman in F-111F and other US Air Force combat aircraft types).

Index